D1179925

COOK'S KITCHEN

Slow Cooking

igloobooks

Published in 2014
by Igloo Books Ltd
Cottage Farm
Sywell
NN6 0BJ
www.igloobooks.com

Food photography and recipe development: PhotoCuisine UK
Front and back cover images © PhotoCuisine UK

OCE001 0714
2 4 6 8 10 9 7 5 3 1
ISBN 978-1-78343-532-6

Printed and manufactured in China

Contents

Soups

Squash and Pine Nut Soup

SERVES 6

PREPARATION TIME 10 MINUTES

COOKING TIME 4 HOURS

INGREDIENTS

1 large butternut squash, peeled, deseeded
   and cut into chunks

1 onion, finely chopped

2 cloves of garlic, finely chopped

1 tsp ground cumin

1 litre / 1 pint 15 fl. oz / 4 cups vegetable stock

3 tbsp pine nuts

2 tbsp chives, chopped

salt and pepper

METHOD

- Mix the squash with the onion, garlic and cumin in a slow cooker, then pour over the stock and season with salt and pepper.

- Cover the slow cooker and cook on high for 4 hours. Use a potato masher or stick blender to break down the squash into a purée.

- Toast the pine nuts in a dry frying pan for 2 minutes or until golden, stirring frequently.

- Ladle the soup into warm bowls then sprinkle with the pine nuts and chives.

TOP TIP

This soup is also delicious made with sweet potatoes.

Slow-cooked Spring Vegetable Minestrone

SERVES 4

PREPARATION TIME 5 MINUTES

COOKING TIME 1 HOUR 30 MINUTES

INGREDIENTS

1.2 litres / 2 pints / 4 ¾ cups vegetable stock

100 g / 3 ½ oz / 1 cup dried spaccatelle or
   similar pasta shapes

12 asparagus spears, cut into short lengths

1 courgette (zucchini), sliced

4 spring onions (scallions), chopped

2 medium tomatoes, peeled and chopped

3 tbsp pesto

50 g / ¾ oz / piece of Parmesan

METHOD

- Put the stock, pasta, asparagus and courgette in a slow cooker and cook on medium for 1 hour 30 minutes.

- Stir in the tomatoes and pesto, then ladle into warm bowls and shave the Parmesan over the top with a vegetable peeler.

TOP TIP
Try stirring sliced smoked salmon through the soup just before serving.

Summer Vegetable Minestrone

SERVES 4
PREPARATION TIME 5 MINUTES
COOKING TIME 1 HOUR 30 MINUTES

INGREDIENTS

1 onion, chopped

2 cloves of garlic, sliced

1 yellow pepper, deseeded and diced

1 courgette (zucchini) , diced

4 medium tomatoes, peeled and chopped

2 tbsp concentrated tomato purée

100 g / 3 ½ oz / ¾ cup green beans, cut into
    short lengths

100 g / 3 ½ oz / ⅔ cup peas

100 g / 3 ½ oz / 1 cup dried spaghetti, snapped
    into short lengths

1.2 litres / 2 pints / 4 ¾ cups vegetable stock

salt and pepper

METHOD

- Stir everything together in a slow cooker and cook on medium for 2 hours.

- Season to taste with salt and pepper before ladling into warm bowls.

TOP TIP

Stir a spoonful of pesto into each bowl for extra depth of flavour.

Creamy Beetroot Soup

SERVES 4

PREPARATION TIME 15 MINUTES

COOKING TIME 3 HOURS

INGREDIENTS

1.2 litres / 2 pints / 4 ¾ cups vegetable stock

450 g / 1 lb / 3 cups beetroot, peeled and sliced

1 bay leaf

2 tsp cumin seeds, plus extra for sprinkling

150 ml / 5 ½ fl. oz / ⅔ cup double (heavy) cream

salt and pepper

METHOD

- Put the stock, beetroot, bay leaf and cumin seeds in a slow cooker.

- Cover and cook on high for 3 hours. Discard the bay leaf and reserve a few slices of beetroot to garnish, then ladle the rest into a liquidiser and blend until smooth.

- Stir in two thirds of the cream and season to taste with salt and pepper.

- Pour the soup into 4 warm bowls, scatter over the reserved beetroot, drizzle with the rest of the cream and sprinkle with cumin seeds.

TOP TIP

Try garnishing the soup with crumbled feta for a tangy finish.

Haricot and Coriander Soup

SERVES 4

PREPARATION TIME 25 MINUTES

COOKING TIME 8 HOURS

INGREDIENTS

400 g / 14 oz / 2 ⅔ cups dried haricot beans,
    soaked overnight

1 onion, chopped

1 celery stick, chopped

2 tsp coriander (cilantro) seeds, crushed, plus
    extra for sprinkling

4 cloves of garlic, sliced

2 tbsp coriander (cilantro) leaves, chopped

METHOD

- Drain the beans from their soaking water and put them in a large saucepan of cold water. Bring to the boil and cook for 10 minutes, then drain well.

- Mix the beans with the onion, celery, coriander seeds and garlic in a slow cooker. Pour over enough boiling water to cover everything by 5 cm (2 in), then cook on low for 8 hours.

- Season to taste with salt and pepper, then blend until smooth in a liquidiser.

- Ladle into warm bowls and serve garnished with coriander leaves and crushed coriander seeds.

TOP TIP
This soup is also delicious garnished with pieces of crispy bacon.

Carrot and Turkey Soup

SERVES 6

PREPARATION TIME 5 MINUTES

COOKING TIME 4 HOURS

INGREDIENTS

1 small turkey carcass

5 carrots, diced

1 onion, finely chopped

2 cloves of garlic, crushed

4 tbsp crème fraiche

6 wafer thin slices turkey, sliced

½ tsp ground cumin

dill sprigs to garnish

salt and pepper

METHOD

- Put the turkey carcass in a slow cooker, breaking it into pieces if it is too large. Add the carrots, onion and garlic, then pour over enough cold water to cover.

- Cover and cook on low for 4 hours. Remove and discard the turkey bones, then transfer everything to a liquidiser and blend until smooth.

- Season to taste with salt and pepper, then ladle into bowls and top with the crème fraiche and turkey slices. Sprinkle with cumin and garnish with dill sprigs.

TOP TIP
This soup is also delicious spiced with caraway instead of cumin.

Minestrone with Turkey

SERVES 4

PREPARATION TIME 10 MINUTES

COOKING TIME 1 HOUR 30 MINUTES

INGREDIENTS

1.2 litres / 2 pints / 4 ¾ cups turkey stock

100 g / 3 ½ oz / 1 cup dried gomiti or similar
   pasta shapes

4 runner beans, chopped

200 g / 7 oz / 1 ⅓ cups broad beans

100 g / 3 ½ oz / ⅔ cup peas

2 tbsp pesto

25 g / 1 oz / ¼ cup piece of Pecorino

4 slices turkey ham, torn into pieces

salt and pepper

METHOD

- Put the stock, pasta, beans and
  peas in a slow cooker and cook on
  medium for 1 hour 30 minutes.

- Add salt and pepper to taste, then
  ladle into warm bowls. Add half a
  tablespoon of pesto to each bowl,
  then use a vegetable peeler to shave
  over the Pecorino. Garnish with
  turkey ham and serve immediately.

TOP TIP
Try using small strips
of prosciutto instead of
the turkey ham.

Wonton Soup

SERVES 6
PREPARATION TIME 45 MINUTES
COOKING TIME 6 HOURS 30 MINUTES

INGREDIENTS

1 chicken carcass
8 spring onions (scallions), roughly chopped
5 cm (2 in) piece fresh root ginger, sliced
1 lemongrass stem, roughly chopped
dark soy sauce to taste
3 heads pak choi, quartered
coriander (cilantro) leaves to garnish

FOR THE WONTONS

150 g / 5 ½ oz / 1 cup minced chicken
75 g / 2 ½ oz / ½ cup raw prawns, finely
    chopped
2 cloves of garlic, crushed
1 tsp fresh root ginger, finely grated
2 spring onions (scallions), finely chopped
1 red chilli (chili), finely chopped
2 tbsp coriander (cilantro), finely chopped
1 tbsp light soy sauce
24 wonton wrappers

METHOD

- Put the chicken carcass, spring onions, ginger and lemon grass in a slow cooker and add enough cold water to cover. Cover and cook on low for 6 hours, then pass the broth through a coffee filter lined sieve to clarify. Season to taste with dark soy sauce.

- While the broth is cooking, mix the minced chicken with the prawns, garlic, ginger, spring onion, chilli and coriander. Stir in the soy sauce. Divide the filling between the wonton wrappers, then fold them in half and press firmly to seal. Fold the edges round and crimp together.

- Wash and dry the slow cooker and pour in the broth. Cook on high until it starts to simmer, then add the wontons and pak choi. Cover and cook for 15 minutes or until the wontons have all started to float and the pak choi stalks are just tender.

- Ladle into warm bowls and garnish with coriander leaves.

TOP TIP
You can also use fresh scallops in place of the prawns.

Mussel Chowder

SERVES 4

PREPARATION TIME 15 MINUTES

COOKING TIME 1 HOUR

INGREDIENTS

2 shallots, finely chopped

2 cloves of garlic, crushed

175 ml / 6 fl. oz / ⅔ cup dry white wine

1.2 litres / 2 pints / 4 ¾ cups live mussels,
    scrubbed

500 ml / 17 ½ fl. oz / 2 cups fish stock

250 ml / 9 fl. oz / 1 cup double (heavy) cream

1 tbsp flat leaf parsley, chopped

salt and pepper

METHOD

- Put all of the ingredients except for the cream and parsley in a slow cooker and cook on medium for 1 hour.

- Scoop out the mussels with a slotted spoon and place in a bowl. Stir the cream into the slow cooker, cover and continue to cook. Meanwhile, pick the mussel meat from the shells, leaving a few whole for a garnish.

- Stir the mussel meat into the soup and season to taste with salt and pepper. Ladle into warm bowls and garnish with the parsley and reserved mussels in their shells.

TOP TIP
Try using a mixture of clams and mussels.

Lettuce Soup

SERVES 6

PREPARATION TIME 5 MINUTES

COOKING TIME 1 HOUR

INGREDIENTS

1.2 litres / 2 pints / 5 cups vegetable stock
1 iceberg lettuce, chopped
1 carrot, coarsely grated
100 g / 3 ½ oz / 1 ⅓ cups button mushrooms,
    sliced
a small bunch of chives, cut into short lengths
salt and pepper

METHOD

- Stir everything together in a slow cooker, then cook on low for 1 hour.

- Taste the soup for seasoning and adjust with salt and pepper, then ladle into bowls and serve.

TOP TIP
This soup also tastes great served chilled in the summer.

French Onion Soup

SERVES 4
PREPARATION TIME 10 MINUTES
COOKING TIME 7 HOURS

INGREDIENTS

2 tbsp butter
3 onions, quartered and sliced
2 cloves of garlic, sliced
1 tbsp balsamic vinegar
1 tbsp runny honey
1 tbsp plain (all purpose) flour
125 ml/ 4 ½ fl. oz / ½ cup dark ale
1 litre / 1 pint 15 fl. oz / 4 cups vegetable stock
salt and pepper

METHOD

- Put the butter in a slow cooker and cook on high until it melts. Stir in the onions, garlic, balsamic and honey and season well with salt and pepper. Cover and cook on high for 1 hour, stirring every 15 minutes.

- Stir in the flour, then gradually incorporate the ale and stock, stirring as you go to eliminate any lumps. Cover and cook on low for 6 hours.

- Taste the soup for seasoning and adjust with salt and pepper, then ladle into warm bowls and serve.

TOP TIP
Top the bread with gruyère and melt under a hot grill.

Curried Lentil Soup

SERVES 6

PREPARATION TIME 5 MINUTES

COOKING TIME 3 HOURS 10 MINUTES

INGREDIENTS

tbsp mustard oil, plus extra for drizzling

onions, finely chopped

cloves of garlic, crushed

5 cm (1 in) piece fresh root ginger, grated

tbsp curry powder

00 g / 14 oz / 3 ¼ cups red lentils

2 litres / 2 pints / 5 cups vegetable stock

oriander (cilantro) leaves to garnish

lt and pepper

METHOD

- Heat the oil in a frying pan and fry the onion, garlic and ginger over a medium heat for 10 minutes to soften without colouring. Stir in the curry powder and cook for 1 more minute, then scrape the contents of the pan into a slow cooker and stir in the lentils and stock.

- Cover and cook on high for 3 hours or until the lentils are very soft. Transfer the soup to a liquidiser and blend until smooth, then season with salt and pepper.

- Ladle the soup into warm bowls then drizzle with mustard oil and garnish with coriander.

TOP TIP

Try serving the soup with fresh naan bread for dunking.

Prawn and Noodle Broth

SERVES 4
PREPARATION TIME 15 MINUTES
COOKING TIME 2 HOURS 15 MINUTES

INGREDIENTS

300 g / 10 ½ oz / 2 cups raw king prawns
3 tbsp dried black Chinese mushrooms
2 tbsp Thai green curry paste
1 red chilli (chili), sliced
1 tbsp fish sauce
1 tsp caster (superfine) sugar
200 g / 7 oz / 1 ½ cups fresh egg noodles
100 g / 3 ½ oz / ¾ cup sugar snap peas

METHOD

- Peel the prawns, leaving the tails intact, then put the heads and shells in a slow cooker with the fungus. Pour in 1 litre of water, then cover and cook on medium for 2 hours.

- Strain the stock, then return it to the pan with the mushrooms, discarding the heads and shells.

- Turn the heat to high and stir in the curry paste, chilli, fish sauce and caster sugar. Taste the broth and adjust with extra fish sauce or sugar accordingly.

- Add the noodles and sugar snaps to the pan, then cover and cook for 5 minutes. Add the prawns then cover and cook for 2 minutes or until they are just opaque. Ladle into bowls and serve.

TOP TIP
For a gluten-free alternative, replace the egg noodles with rice noodles.

Tomato and Leek Soup

SERVES 4

PREPARATION TIME 15 MINUTES

COOKING TIME 3 HOURS 30 MINUTES

INGREDIENTS

- tbsp olive oil
- leeks, finely chopped
- cloves of garlic, crushed
- tbsp concentrated tomato purée
- 00 g / 14 oz / 2 cups ripe tomatoes, chopped
- litre / 1 pint 15 fl. oz / 4 cups vegetable stock
- tbsp flat leaf parsley, chopped
- alt and pepper

METHOD

- Heat the oil in a slow cooker set to high. Reserve 2 tbsp of the leek for a garnish and stir the rest into the oil with the garlic. Season with salt and pepper, then cover and cook for 30 minutes, stirring every 10 minutes.

- Stir in the tomato purée, tomatoes and stock, then cover and cook on low for 3 hours.

- Transfer the soup to a liquidiser and blend until smooth, then pass the soup through a sieve to remove any seeds and bits of skin.

- Taste for seasoning then ladle the soup into warm bowls. Mix the reserved leek with the parsley and sprinkle on top.

TOP TIP

Add two chopped red peppers before cooking for a more savoury flavour.

Leek, Potato and Bacon Soup

SERVES 4

PREPARATION TIME 25 MINUTES

COOKING TIME 6 HOURS

INGREDIENTS

1 ham bone

2 leeks, finely chopped

450 g / 1 lb / 2 cups potatoes, peeled
and cubed

2 cloves of garlic, crushed

8 rashers back bacon

100 ml / 3 ½ fl. oz / ½ cup double (heavy)
cream

baby chard to garnish

salt and pepper

METHOD

- Put the ham bone in a slow cooker and pour over enough cold water to cover.

- Cover and cook on low for 4 hours. Remove and discard the bone, then stir in the leeks, potato and garlic. Cover and cook on medium for 2 hours.

- Towards the end of the cooking time, grill the bacon for 2 minutes on each side or until crisp.

- Transfer the soup to a liquidiser and blend until smooth. Season to taste with salt and pepper. Transfer 100 ml / 3 ½ fl. oz / ½ cup to a small measuring jug and add the cream. Use an stick blender at a slight angle to aerate the mixture until it forms a creamy foam.

- Pour the soup into warm bowls and spoon over the foam. Garnish with baby chard and black pepper and serve with the crispy bacon.

TOP TIP
Stir in ½ tsp of ground cumin at the end for a delicious savoury soup.

Japanese Prawn and Noodle Soup

SERVES 4

PREPARATION TIME 20 MINUTES

COOKING TIME 2 HOURS 10 MINUTES

INGREDIENTS

300 g / 10 ½ oz / 2 cups raw king prawns
15 g / ½ oz / ⅛ cup piece of kombu
4 tbsp dried bonito flakes
200 g / 7 oz / 2 cups fresh rice noodles
2 spring onions (scallions), thinly sliced
2 mild red chillies (chilies), thinly sliced
2 tbsp coriander (cilantro) leaves

METHOD

- Peel the prawns and put the heads and shells in a slow cooker. Pour in 1 litre / 1 pint 15 fl. oz / 4 cups of water, then cover and cook on medium for 2 hours.

- Stir in the kombu and bonito flakes, then cover and cook for 5 minutes.

- Strain the stock, then return it to the pan and stir in the noodles and prawns. Cover and cook for 3 minutes or until the prawns just turn opaque.

- Ladle the soup into warm bowls and garnish with spring onion, chilli and coriander.

TOP TIP

This soup is also delicious made with fresh egg noodles.

Fennel and Courgette Soup

SERVES 6

PREPARATION TIME 30 MINUTES

COOKING TIME 4 HOURS

INGREDIENTS

2 fennel bulbs, chopped with fronds reserved
2 courgettes (zucchinis), chopped
1 onion, finely chopped
2 cloves of garlic, finely chopped
1 tsp ground fennel seeds
1 litre / 1 pint 15 fl. oz / 4 cups vegetable stock
50 g / 1 ¾ oz / ½ cup Parmesan, grated
salt and pepper

METHOD

- Mix the fennel with the courgette, onion, garlic and fennel seeds in a slow cooker, then pour over the stock.

- Cover the slow cooker and cook on high for 4 hours. Transfer the soup to a liquidiser and blend until smooth, then season to taste with salt and pepper.

- Heat the oven to 180°C (160°C fan) / 350F / gas 4. Use a round cookie cutter to shape the Parmesan into 6 rounds on a non-stick baking tray. Transfer the tray to the oven and cook for 3 minutes or until the cheese has melted. Leave to cool and harden on the tray for a few minutes, then lift off with a palette knife.

- Pour the soup into warm bowls and garnish with the reserved fennel fronds. Serve with the Parmesan crisps.

TOP TIP
This soup is also delicious served chilled and garnished with crumbled feta.

Creamy Cauliflower and Broccoli Soup

SERVES 4

PREPARATION TIME 15 MINUTES

COOKING TIME 3 HOURS

INGREDIENTS

1.2 litres / 2 pints / 4 ¾ cups vegetable stock

1 head of broccoli, chopped

1 cauliflower, chopped

1 bay leaf

150 ml / 5 ½ fl. oz / ⅔ cup double (heavy) cream

50 g / 1 ¾ oz / ½ cup piece of Parmesan

nutmeg for grating

salt and pepper

METHOD

- Put the stock, broccoli, cauliflower and bay leaf in a slow cooker.

- Cover and cook on low for 3 hours. Discard the bay leaf then ladle the soup into a liquidiser and blend until smooth.

- Stir in most the cream and season to taste with salt and pepper.

- Pour the soup into 4 warm bowls, drizzle over the remaining cream, then use a vegetable peeler to shave the Parmesan over the top. Finely grate a little nutmeg over the top and serve.

TOP TIP

Garnish with crumbled Stilton in place of the Parmesan.

Pumpkin and Rosemary Soup

SERVES 6

PREPARATION TIME 10 MINUTES

COOKING TIME 4 HOURS

INGREDIENTS

600 g / 1 lb 5 ½ oz / 3 cups pumpkin, peeled,
    deseeded and cut into chunks
1 onion, finely chopped
2 cloves of garlic, finely chopped
3 sprigs rosemary, plus extra to garnish
1 litre / 1 pint 15 fl. oz / 4 cups vegetable stock
2 slices stale crusty bread
salt and pepper

METHOD

- Mix the pumpkin with the onion, garlic and rosemary in a slow cooker, then pour over the stock and season with salt and pepper.

- Cover the slow cooker and cook on high for 4 hours. Remove and discard the rosemary, then transfer the soup to a liquidiser and blend until smooth. Taste the soup and adjust the seasoning.

- Pour the soup into warm bowls. Tear the bread into rough croutons and scatter on top, then garnish with fresh rosemary.

TOP TIP
This soup also works really well with sweet potato in place of the pumpkin.

Pea and Ham Soup

SERVES 8

PREPARATION TIME 5 MINUTES

COOKING TIME 8 HOURS

INGREDIENTS

ham hock
00 g / 14 oz / 3 ¼ cups green split peas
onion, finely chopped
cloves of garlic, crushed
bay leaf
lt and pepper

METHOD

- Put all of the ingredients in a slow cooker and pour over 2 litres / 4 pints 2 fl. oz / 8 cups of water.

- Cover and cook on high for 8 hours. Discard the bay leaf, then remove the ham hock from the soup and shred the meat off the bone.

- Use an stick blender to purée most of the split peas, leaving some whole for texture. Stir in the shredded ham and taste for seasoning, then ladle into warm bowls and serve.

TOP TIP

Stir a handful of fresh peas through the soup 10 minutes before the end.

Main Meals

Bouillabaisse

SERVES 4

PREPARATION TIME 30 MINUTES

COOKING TIME 6 HOURS 10 MINUTES

INGREDIENTS

sea bass

gurnard

300 g / 10 ½ oz / 2 cups raw king prawns

langoustines

tbsp olive oil

onion, finely chopped

celery stick, finely chopped

carrot, finely chopped

cloves of garlic, crushed

tbsp Pernod

tomato, diced

pinch of saffron

450 g / 1 lb / 2 ¼ cups live mussels, scrubbed

tbsp flat leaf parsley, chopped

salt and pepper

METHOD

- Fillet the fish and put the heads and bones in a slow cooker. Peel the prawns, keeping the tails intact, and add the heads to the slow cooker along with the langoustine heads.

- Heat the oil in a frying pan and fry the onion, celery, carrot and garlic for 5 minutes without colouring. Pour in the Pernod and bubble until almost evaporated, then scrape the contents of the pan into the slow cooker with the chopped tomato and saffron.

- Pour in enough cold water to cover everything by 2.5 cm (1 in), then cover and cook on low for 6 hours.

- Transfer the contents of the slow cooker to a liquidiser and blend until smooth, then pass the mixture through a sieve back into the slow cooker.

- Cut the fish fillets into chunks and stir into the soup with the mussels, prawns and langoustines. Cover and cook on medium for 10 minutes or until the mussels open. Season to taste with salt and pepper, then ladle into bowls and serve garnished with parsley.

TOP TIP

Chill the soup overnight and reheat the next day.

Pot-roasted Guinea Fowl

SERVES 2
PREPARATION TIME 15 MINUTES
COOKING TIME 45 MINUTES

INGREDIENTS

2 tbsp olive oil

2 guinea fowl leg quarters

1 leek, halved and sliced

1 carrot, diced

8 baby turnips, peeled

100 g / 3 ½ oz / 2 cups oyster mushrooms, torn into strips

2 sprigs fresh sage, plus extra to garnish

200 ml / 7 fl. oz / ¾ cup dry cider

METHOD

- Preheat the oven to 180°C (160°C fan) / 350F / gas 4.

- Heat the oil in a frying pan. Season the guinea fowl well with salt and pepper, then sear on all sides until nicely browned.

- Divide the leek, carrots, turnips, mushrooms and sage between 2 individual casserole dishes, then lay the guinea fowl legs on top.

- Pour over the cider, then cover the dishes and bake them in the oven for 45 minutes. Insert a skewer into the thickest part of the thigh – if the juice runs clear, the meat is cooked.

- Garnish the dishes with fresh sage and serve immediately.

TOP TIP

If you can't source guinea fowl, use chicken instead.

Stewed Peppers and Tomatoes

SERVES 4

PREPARATION TIME 5 MINUTES

COOKING TIME 2 HOURS 30 MINUTES

INGREDIENTS

3 tbsp olive oil

1 onion, sliced

2 red peppers, deseeded and cut into chunks

2 yellow peppers, deseeded and cut into chunks

2 green peppers, deseeded and cut into chunks

2 cloves of garlic, sliced

4 medium tomatoes

4 tbsp dry sherry

250 ml / 9 fl. oz / 1 cup vegetable stock

salt and pepper

METHOD

- Put the oil in a slow cooker and heat on high. Stir in the onion and peppers and season with salt and pepper. Cover and cook for 1 hour 30 minutes, stirring every 15 minutes.

- Stir in the garlic, tomatoes and sherry, then pour over the vegetable stock.

- Cover and cook on low for 2 hours. Season to taste before serving.

TOP TIP

Poach eggs directly into the stew — cook until the whites are set with the yolks still runny.

Lamb, Courgette and Aubergine Tagine

SERVES 4

PREPARATION TIME 10 MINUTES

COOKING TIME 2 HOURS 15 MINUTES

INGREDIENTS

450 g / 1 lb / 3 cups lamb shoulder, cubed
2 tsp ras el hanout spice mix
2 cinnamon sticks
2 tbsp olive oil
2 tbsp honey
1 onion, diced
1 courgette (zucchini), sliced
½ aubergine (eggplant), cut into chunks
1 red pepper, deseeded and cut into chunks
50 g / 1 ¾ oz / ¼ cup sultanas
250 ml / 9 fl. oz / 1 cup good quality lamb stock
2 tbsp flat leaf parsley, chopped
1 tbsp mint leaves, chopped
sea salt

METHOD

- Preheat the oven to 160°C (140°C fan) / 325F / gas 3.

- Put the lamb, spices, oil, honey, vegetables and sultanas in a large tagine with a big pinch of salt and stir well to mix.

- Pour over the stock then put on the lid and transfer the tagine to the oven.

- Cook the tagine for 2 hours, then remove the lid, stir well and cook for another 15 minutes. Sprinkle with parsley and mint just before serving.

TOP TIP
For a more piquant taste, use capers instead of sultanas.

Salmon, Carrot and Olive Tagine

SERVES 4

PREPARATION TIME 10 MINUTES

COOKING TIME 1 HOUR 30 MINUTES

INGREDIENTS

3 carrots, peeled and sliced

2 tomatoes, halved

½ preserved lemon, sliced

1 onion, chopped

a pinch of saffron

250 ml / 9 fl. oz / 1 cup good quality fish stock

4 portions of salmon fillet

100 g / 3 ½ oz / ⅔ cup green olives

2 tbsp olive oil

1 tbsp flat leaf parsley, chopped

METHOD

- Preheat the oven to 160°C (140°C fan) / 325F / gas 3.

- Mix the carrots, tomatoes, preserved lemon and onion together in a tagine. Stir the saffron into the stock and pour it over the vegetables, then put on the lid and bake for 1 hour.

- Arrange the salmon and olives on top of the vegetables and drizzle with the oil. Cover the tagine and return it to the oven, then turn the temperature down to 140°C (120°C fan) / 275F / gas 1.

- Cook the tagine for another 30 minutes, then sprinkle with parsley and serve.

TOP TIP
This tagine also works really well with swordfish.

Squash and Chestnut Tagine

SERVES 4

PREPARATION TIME 10 MINUTES

COOKING TIME 3 HOURS

INGREDIENTS

1 butternut squash, peeled, deseeded and cut
  into chunks

12 chestnuts, peeled

8 pieces cassia bark

2.5 cm (1 in) piece root ginger, finely chopped

3 cloves of garlic, finely chopped

1 tsp ground cumin

1 tsp ground coriander (cilantro)

2 tbsp olive oil

400 ml / 14 fl. oz / 1 ⅔ cups vegetable stock

coriander (cilantro) to garnish

salt and pepper

METHOD

- Preheat the oven to 150°C (130°C fan) / 300F / gas 2.

- Divide the squash and chestnuts between 4 individual tagines and top with the cassia bark. Stir the ginger, garlic, cumin, coriander and oil into the stock and season well with salt and pepper, then pour it over the vegetables.

- Put the lids on the tagines and transfer them to the oven. Bake for 3 hours or until the squash and chestnuts are tender. Garnish with coriander before serving.

TOP TIP
This recipe tastes great made with sweet potato too.

Chicken and Preserved Lemon Tagine

ERVES 4

REPARATION TIME 15 MINUTES

OOKING TIME 2 HOURS

INGREDIENTS

tbsp olive oil

chicken, jointed

onion, diced

cloves of garlic, sliced

tsp ground coriander (cilantro)

tsp ground ginger

preserved lemon, sliced

00 g / 3 ½ oz / ⅔ cup kalamata olives

50 ml / 9 fl. oz / 1 cup chicken stock

oriander (cilantro) to garnish

ea salt

METHOD

- Preheat the oven to 160°C (140°C fan) / 325F / gas 3.

- Heat the oil in a large frying pan and season the chicken with salt. Sear the chicken pieces on all sides, then transfer to a tagine.

- Add the onion, garlic, spices, preserved lemon and olives to the tagine and mix well. Pour over the stock then put on the lid and transfer the tagine to the oven.

- Cook the tagine for 2 hours, then garnish with coriander and serve.

TOP TIP
Stir a big handful of chopped flat leaf parsley into the tagine at the end.

Braised Haricot Beans

SERVES 6
PREPARATION TIME 15 MINUTES
COOKING TIME 6–8 HOURS

INGREDIENTS

400 g / 14 oz / 2 ⅔ cups dried haricot beans,
    soaked overnight
1 onion, chopped
1 carrot, chopped
4 tomatoes, quartered
4 cloves of garlic, sliced
2 tbsp flat leaf parsley, chopped
salt and pepper

METHOD

- Drain the beans from their soaking water and put them in a large saucepan of cold water. Bring to the boil and cook for 10 minutes, then drain well.

- Mix the beans with the onion, carrot, tomatoes and garlic in a slow cooker. Pour over enough boiling water to cover everything by 5 cm (2 in), then cook on low for 6–8 hours or until the beans are tender, but still holding their shape.

- Season the beans to taste with salt and pepper, then stir in the parsley and serve.

TOP TIP
Try using butterbeans or chickpeas in place of the haricot beans.

Veal Tagine with Pumpkin and Tomatoes

SERVES 4

PREPARATION TIME 20 MINUTES

COOKING TIME 3 HOURS

INGREDIENTS

450 g / 1 lb / 3 cups veal shoulder, cubed

1 tbsp plain (all purpose) flour

1 tbsp olive oil

1 onion, finely chopped

2 cloves of garlic, crushed

2.5 cm (1 in) piece fresh root ginger, finely grated

50 g / 1 ¾ oz / ¼ cup sultanas

1 tsp ras el hanout spice mix

1 tbsp runny honey

1 tbsp coriander (cilantro), chopped, plus extra to garnish

250 ml / 9 fl. oz / 1 cup good quality veal stock

salt and pepper

FOR THE PUMPKIN AND TOMATO

400 g / 14 oz / 3 cups pumpkin, peeled and cubed

1 tbsp olive oil

2 tomatoes, sliced

½ lemon

1 tbsp runny honey

METHOD

- Preheat the oven to 160°C (140°C fan) / 325F / gas 3.

- Season the veal with salt and pepper and dust the pieces with flour to coat. Heat the oil in a large frying pan and sear the veal in batches on all sides.

- Transfer the veal to a tagine and stir in the onion, garlic, ginger, sultanas, ras el hanout, honey and coriander. Season well with salt.

- Pour over the stock then put on the lid and transfer the tagine to the oven. Cook the tagine for 3 hours.

- 1 hour before the end of the cooking time, put the pumpkin in a roasting tin, drizzle with oil and season with salt and pepper. Roast the pumpkin for 45 minutes, stirring half way through. Add the tomatoes to the pan then squeeze over the lemon and drizzle with honey. Return to the oven for 15 minutes.

- Taste the tagine and adjust the seasoning then divide between 4 individual serving tagines. Top with the pumpkin and tomato and garnish with coriander before serving.

TOP TIP
You can replace the veal with pork or turkey breast.

Rabbit, Carrot and Almond Tagine

METHOD

- Preheat the oven to 160°C (140°C fan) / 325F / gas 3.

- Divide the rabbit pieces, carrots, onion, garlic and preserved lemon between 2 individual tagines. Stir the ras el hanout, oil and honey into the stock and season with salt, then pour it over the rabbit.

- Put the lids on the tagines and transfer them to the oven, then bake for 1 hour 30 minutes.

- Remove the lids and sprinkle with almonds, then return to the oven for 15 minutes to brown the tops. Sprinkle with thyme and serve immediately.

SERVES 2

PREPARATION TIME 10 MINUTES

COOKING TIME 1 HOUR 45 MINUTES

INGREDIENTS

1 rabbit, jointed

4 baby carrots, halved lengthways

1 red onion, cut into wedges

3 cloves of garlic, finely chopped

2 slices preserved lemon

1 tsp ras el hanout spice mix

2 tbsp olive oil

2 tbsp runny honey

250 ml / 9 fl. oz / 1 cup chicken stock

2 tbsp flaked (slivered) almonds

1 tsp thyme leaves

TOP TIP

This tagine is also delicious made with whole quail.

Beef, Pepper and Olive Stew

SERVES 4

PREPARATION TIME 15 MINUTES

COOKING TIME 6 HOURS

INGREDIENTS

450 g / 1 lb / 3 cups stewing beef, cubed

2 tbsp plain (all purpose) flour

2 tbsp olive oil

1 red pepper, deseeded and cut into wedges

1 yellow pepper, deseeded and cut into wedges

1 green pepper, deseeded and cut into wedges

150 g / 5 ½ oz / 1 cup green olives, pitted

1 onion, finely chopped

3 cloves of garlic, crushed

2 tbsp concentrated tomato purée

2 bay leaves

a few sprigs of thyme

500 ml / 17 ½ fl. oz / 2 cups good quality beef stock

couscous to serve

salt and pepper

METHOD

- Preheat the oven to 160°C (140°C fan) / 325F / gas 3.

- Season the beef with salt and pepper and dust the pieces with flour to coat. Heat the oil in a large frying pan and sear the beef in batches on all sides.

- Transfer the beef to a slow cooker and stir in the rest of the ingredients. Season well with salt and pepper.

- Put the lid on the slow cooker and cook on low for 6 hours, stirring every 2 hours. Serve with couscous.

TOP TIP
You can also make this stew with lamb instead of beef.

Beef, Turnip and Lardon Stew

SERVES 4

PREPARATION TIME 20 MINUTES

COOKING TIME 6 HOURS

INGREDIENTS

450 g / 1 lb / 3 cups stewing beef, cubed

2 tbsp plain (all purpose) flour

2 tbsp olive oil

100 g / 2 ⅓ oz / ½ cup lardons

6 small turnips, peeled and halved

125 ml / 4 ½ fl. oz / ½ cup red wine

1 onion, finely chopped

3 cloves of garlic, crushed

2 bay leaves

½ orange, zest pared into thin strips

500 ml / 17 ½ fl. oz / 2 cups good quality beef stock

salt and pepper

METHOD

- Season the beef with salt and pepper and dust the pieces with flour to coat. Heat the oil in a large frying pan and sear the beef in batches on all sides.

- Transfer the beef to a slow cooker, then fry the lardons and turnips until lightly coloured. Deglaze the pan with the wine, then tip everything into the slow cooker and stir in the rest of the ingredients. Season well with salt and pepper.

- Put the lid on the slow cooker and cook on low for 6 hours, stirring every 2 hours.

TOP TIP
Try using stout instead of the red wine for a more savoury flavour.

Lamb Stew with Spring Vegetables

SERVES 4

PREPARATION TIME 20 MINUTES

COOKING TIME 5 HOURS 30 MINUTES

INGREDIENTS

thick slices lamb neck, on the bone

tbsp plain (all purpose) flour

tbsp olive oil

125 ml / 4 ½ fl. oz / ½ cup white wine

2 new potatoes, scrubbed

leeks, cut into chunks

2 baby carrots, scrubbed

500 ml / 17 ½ fl. oz / 2 cups good quality lamb stock

runner beans, halved and sliced lengthways

tbsp kalamata olives

flat leaf parsley to garnish

salt and pepper

METHOD

- Preheat the oven to 160°C (140°C fan) / 325F / gas 3.

- Season the lamb with salt and pepper and dust with flour to coat. Heat the oil in a large frying pan and sear the lamb on all sides.

- Transfer the lamb to a slow cooker, then deglaze the pan with the wine and scrape it in with the lamb. Add the potatoes, leeks, carrots and stock to the slow cooker and season well with salt and pepper.

- Put the lid on the slow cooker and cook on low for 5 hours. Stir in the beans and olives, then cover and cook for another 30 minutes. Serve garnished with parsley.

TOP TIP
You can also use oxtail in place of the lamb neck.

Braised Mince and Beans

SERVES 8

PREPARATION TIME 15 MINUTES

COOKING TIME 6–8 HOURS

INGREDIENTS

2 tbsp olive oil

450 g / 1 lb / 3 cups minced beef

400 g / 14 oz / 2 ⅔ cups dried borlotti beans,
    soaked overnight

1 onion, finely chopped

4 cloves of garlic, crushed

1 carrot, finely chopped

4 tomatoes, finely chopped

2 tbsp concentrated tomato purée

salt and pepper

METHOD

- Heat the oil in a frying pan and brown the mince.

- Drain the beans from their soaking water and put them in a large saucepan of cold water. Bring to the boil and cook for 10 minutes, then drain well.

- Mix everything together in a slow cooker, then pour over enough boiling water to cover everything by 5 cm (2 in). Cook on low for 6–8 hours or until the beans are tender, but still holding their shape.

- Season the beans to taste with salt and pepper before serving.

TOP TIP
For a vegetarian alternative, use vegetarian mince.

Veal Blanquette

SERVES 4

PREPARATION TIME 5 MINUTES

COOKING TIME 4 HOURS 30 MINUTES

INGREDIENTS

tbsp butter

00 g / 1 lb 12 oz / 4 cups veal shoulder, cubed

leek, sliced

carrot, chopped

celery stick, chopped

0 g / 7 oz / 1 ⅓ cups baby onions, peeled

0 g / 5 ½ oz / 1 cup baby button mushrooms

0 ml / 1 pint / 2 ½ cups light veal or
  chicken stock

0 ml / 10 ½ fl. oz / 1 ¼ cups double
  (heavy) cream

lt and pepper

METHOD

- Put everything except for the cream in a slow cooker and stir well to mix.

- Cook on low for 4 hours. Stir in the cream and cook on high for 30 minutes.

- Taste the sauce for seasoning and adjust with salt and black pepper.

TOP TIP
You can also use turkey or pork in place of the veal.

Lamb Chops with Tomato Sauce

SERVES 4

PREPARATION TIME 15 MINUTES

COOKING TIME 2 HOURS

INGREDIENTS

4 tbsp olive oil

8 lamb chops

4 rashers back bacon

2 bulbs of fennel, thickly sliced

1 onion, sliced

1 tbsp rosemary leaves

150 g / 5 ½ oz / 2 cups button mushrooms, sliced

100 ml / 3 ½ fl. oz / ½ cup dry white wine

400 ml / 7 fl. oz / 1 ⅔ cups tomato passata

a few sprigs of basil

METHOD

- Heat the oil in a frying pan and sear the lamb chops on both sides, followed by the bacon. Transfer to a slow cooker and add the rest of the ingredients.

- Cover and cook on high for 2 hours, then garnish with basil and serve.

TOP TIP

Try using pork chops in place of the lamb chops.

Prawn Bisque

SERVES 6

PREPARATION TIME 15 MINUTES

COOKING TIME 3 HOURS 45 MINUTES

INGREDIENTS

- 450 g / 1 lb / 3 cups small shell-on prawns (shrimps)
- 1 fennel bulb, diced
- 1 onion, diced
- 6 cloves of garlic, unpeeled
- 4 medium tomatoes, quartered
- 3 tbsp olive oil
- 3 tbsp brandy
- 1 litre / 1 pint 15 fl. oz / 4 cups fish stock
- 2 tbsp concentrated tomato purée
- 4 tbsp double (heavy) cream
- 12 large shell-on king prawns
- salt and pepper

METHOD

- Preheat the oven to 220°C (200°C fan) / 425F / gas 7.

- Spread out the prawns, fennel, onion, garlic and tomatoes in a roasting tin. Drizzle with oil and season with salt and pepper, then roast for 15 minutes.

- Stir the brandy into the tin, then scrape everything into a slow cooker and stir in the fish stock and tomato purée. Cover and cook on medium for 3 hours.

- Transfer the contents of the slow cooker to a liquidiser and blend until smooth. Pass the bisque through a sieve back into the slow cooker. Stir in the cream and add the king prawns, then cover and cook on low for 30 minutes.

- Taste the bisque and adjust the seasoning before serving.

TOP TIP

You can use this method to make crab bisque too, but don't use the hard carapice.

Pork and Rosemary Stew

SERVES 4

PREPARATION TIME 10 MINUTES

COOKING TIME 4 HOURS 30 MINUTES

INGREDIENTS

2 tbsp butter

800 g / 1 lb 12 oz / 5 ⅓ cups pork shoulder, cubed

1 onion, finely chopped

1 celery stick, finely chopped

4 medium potatoes, peeled and cubed

1 bay leaf

4 sprigs of rosemary

600 ml / 1 pint / 2 ½ cups chicken stock

300 ml / 10 ½ fl. oz / 1 ¼ cups double (heavy) cream

2 tsp grain mustard

METHOD

- Heat the butter in a large frying pan and sear the pork on all sides. Transfer the pork to a slow cooker and stir in the rest of the ingredients, except for the cream and mustard.

- Cover and cook on low for 4 hours.

- Stir in the cream and mustard and cook on high for 30 minutes. Taste the sauce for seasoning and adjust with salt and black pepper.

TOP TIP

Try adding chopped Greek beans 15 minutes before the end of the cooking time.

Vegetable Tagine

SERVES 4

PREPARATION TIME 5 MINUTES

COOKING TIME 2 HOURS

INGREDIENTS

courgettes (zucchinis), cut into chunks

aubergine (eggplant), cut into chunks

red pepper, deseeded and cut into chunks

onion, finely chopped

cloves of garlic, finely chopped

00 g / 14 oz / 1 ¾ cups canned tomatoes, chopped

tsp ras el hanout spice mix

tbsp thyme leaves

alt and pepper

METHOD

- Preheat the oven to 160°C (140°C fan) / 325F / gas 3.

- Stir everything together in a large tagine with a big pinch of salt. Cover the tagine with its lid and transfer to the oven.

- Cook the tagine for 2 hours, then taste and adjust the seasoning before serving.

TOP TIP

Try adding a handful of capers for a great piquant taste.

Mini Casseroles of Duck and Prawns

SERVES 4

PREPARATION TIME 5 MINUTES

COOKING TIME 1 HOUR

INGREDIENTS

1 duck breast, thinly sliced

16 raw king prawns, peeled

1 courgette (zucchini), diced

2.5 cm (1 in) piece fresh root ginger, julienned

1 clove of garlic, crushed

2 tbsp Shaoxing rice wine

2 tbsp light soy sauce

2 tsp runny honey

1 tbsp sesame seeds

1 tbsp coriander (cilantro), chopped

METHOD

- Preheat the oven to 160°C (140°C fan) / 325F / gas 3.

- Toss the duck with the prawns, courgette, ginger and garlic and divide between 4 mini casserole dishes. Stir the rice wine, soy and honey together and drizzle over the top.

- Put the lids on the casseroles then transfer to the oven and bake for 1 hour.

- Sprinkle with sesame seeds and coriander before serving.

TOP TIP

Try adding a chopped red pepper.

Pot au Feu

SERVES 4
PREPARATION TIME 20 MINUTES
COOKING TIME 8 HOURS

INGREDIENTS

450 g / 1 lb / 3 cups beef brisket
ham bone
small turnips, scrubbed
salad onions, peeled
carrots, peeled
cloves of garlic, sliced
bay leaves

METHOD

- Put all of the ingredients in a slow cooker and pour over enough water to cover by 2.5 cm (1 in).

- Cover and cook on low for 8 hours. Cut the beef into chunks or slices and serve with the vegetables and cooking liquor.

TOP TIP
Serve with plenty of crusty bread.

Pot-roasted Quail with Pears

SERVES 2
PREPARATION TIME 10 MINUTES
COOKING TIME 1 HOUR 30 MINUTES

INGREDIENTS

2 tbsp olive oil
2 oven-ready quail
2 pears, peeled and quartered
2 tsp mixed peppercorns
2 cloves
1 tbsp sultanas
1 lemon, juiced
1 tbsp runny honey

METHOD

- Preheat the oven to 160°C (140°C fan) / 325F / gas 3.

- Heat the oil in a frying pan and sear the quail on all sides.

- Transfer the quail to a cast iron casserole dish and tuck the pear quarters around them. Sprinkle over the peppercorns, cloves and sultanas, then stir the lemon and honey together and drizzle over the top.

- Put a lid on the dish and transfer to the oven, then cook for 1 hour. Remove the lid and cook for another 30 minutes.

TOP TIP
You can also use this method for cooking partridge when in season.

Chorizo, Potato and Sweetcorn Stew

SERVES 4

PREPARATION TIME 5 MINUTES

COOKING TIME 3 HOURS

INGREDIENTS

250 g / 9 oz / 1 ⅔ cups mini cooking chorizo

1 large potato, cut into wedges

2 corn cobs, cut into thick slices

4 spring onions (scallions), cut into short
   lengths

1 chipotle chilli (chili)

200 ml / 7 fl. oz / 1 ⅔ cups tomato passata

1 lime, cut into chunks

1 tbsp coriander (cilantro), chopped

METHOD

- Mix all of the ingredients together,
  except for the lime and coriander, in
  a slow cooker.

- Cover and cook on medium for
  3 hours or until the potatoes are
  tender, but still holding their shape.

- Spoon into warm bowls and garnish
  with lime chunks and coriander.

TOP TIP
This stew is also delicious with the addition of four sliced squid tubes.

95

Chorizo and Lentil Soup

SERVES 6
PREPARATION TIME 5 MINUTES
COOKING TIME 2 HOURS 30 MINUTES

INGREDIENTS

2 tbsp olive oil
225 g / 8 oz / 1 ½ cups chorizo ring, sliced
1 onion, finely chopped
1 celery stick, sliced
2 cloves of garlic, crushed
400 g / 14 oz / 3 ¼ cups red lentils
1.2 litres / 2 pint / 5 cups vegetable stock
1 bay leaf
6 cherry tomatoes, halved
salt and pepper

METHOD

- Heat the oil in a large frying pan and fry the chorizo slices for 1 minute on each side. Transfer to a slow cooker and stir in the rest of the ingredients, except for the tomatoes.

- Cover and cook on high for 2 hours, then stir in the tomatoes and cook for 30 minutes.

- Taste the soup for seasoning and adjust with salt and pepper, then ladle into warm bowls and serve.

TOP TIP
You can also use green lentils to make this soup.

Chicken and Chickpea Tagine

SERVES 4

PREPARATION TIME 15 MINUTES

COOKING TIME 2 HOURS

INGREDIENTS

tbsp olive oil

chicken legs

leek, sliced

carrot, cut into chunks

courgette (zucchini), halved and sliced

150 g / 5 ½ oz / 1 cup canned chickpeas

red chilli (chili), deseeded and chopped

tsp ground cumin

tsp ground coriander (cilantro)

tsp ground ginger

tbsp coriander (cilantro) leaves

250 ml / 9 fl. oz / 1 cup chicken stock

sea salt

METHOD

- Preheat the oven to 160°C (140°C fan) / 325F / gas 3.

- Heat the oil in a large frying pan and season the chicken with salt. Sear the chicken legs on all sides, then transfer to a tagine.

- Mix in the rest of the ingredients, apart from the coriander, then put on the lid and transfer the tagine to the oven.

- Cook the tagine for 2 hours, then garnish with coriander and serve.

TOP TIP

Try using butterbeans in place of the chickpeas.

Mussel and Cauliflower Stew

SERVES 6

PREPARATION TIME 5 MINUTES

COOKING TIME 2 HOURS 15 MINUTES

INGREDIENTS

1.2 litres / 2 pints / 4 ¾ cups fish stock

½ cauliflower, cut into florets

1 large potato, peeled and diced

1 celery stick, sliced

1 leek, sliced

2 bay leaves

2 tbsp flat leaf parsley, chopped

1.2 litres / 2 pints / 4 ¾ cups live mussels, scrubbed

salt and pepper

METHOD

- Put the stock in a slow cooker with the vegetables, bay leaves and half of the parsley. Cover and cook on medium for 2 hours.

- Stir the mussels into the pot, then cover and cook for 15 minutes or until they have all opened. Taste the soup and add salt and pepper as necessary, then sprinkle with parsley and serve.

TOP TIP
Try using clams or cockles instead of the mussels.

Lamb Meatball Tagine

ERVES 4

REPARATION TIME 25 MINUTES

OOKING TIME 2 HOURS

INGREDIENTS

25 g / 8 oz / 1 cup minced lamb

25 g / 8 oz / 1 cup sausagemeat

0 g / 2 oz / ⅔ cup fresh white breadcrumbs

tbsp hummus

tbsp flat leaf parsley, finely chopped

tbsp olive oil

courgettes (zucchini), cut into chunks

large potato, peeled and cut into chunks

carrot, peeled and sliced

onion, quartered and sliced

cloves of garlic, finely chopped

50 g / 5 ½ oz / 1 cup canned chickpeas

50 g / 5 ½ oz / 1 cup peas

00 g / 7 oz / 1 ⅓ cups cherry tomatoes

tsp ras el hanout spice mix

50 ml / 9 fl. oz / 1 cup lamb or vegetable
   stock

alt and pepper

METHOD

- Knead the lamb mince, sausagemeat, breadcrumbs, hummus and parsley together and season with salt and pepper. Shape the mixture into meatballs.

- Heat the oil in a frying pan and sear the meatballs on all sides.

- Preheat the oven to 160°C (140°C fan) / 325F / gas 3.

- Stir everything together in a large tagine with a big pinch of salt. Cover the tagine with its lid and transfer to the oven.

- Cook the tagine for 2 hours, then taste and adjust the seasoning before serving.

TOP TIP

Try serving the tagine with hummus and flatbreads.

Pork and Flageolet Bean Stew

SERVES 8

PREPARATION TIME 10 MINUTES

COOKING TIME 6–8 HOURS

INGREDIENTS

450 g / 1 lb / 3 cups pork shoulder, cut into chunks

400 g / 14 oz / 2 ⅔ cups dried flageolet beans, soaked overnight

1 onion, finely chopped

4 cloves of garlic, crushed

4 medium potatoes, quartered

2 carrots, cut into chunks

400 g / 14 oz / 1 ¾ cups canned tomatoes, chopped

100 g / 3 ½ oz / 2 cups baby leaf spinach

salt and pepper

METHOD

- Drain the beans of their soaking liquid and put into the slow cooker with all the remaining ingredients, apart from the spinach. Add enough water to just cover everything.

- Cover and cook on low for 6–8 hours or until the beans are tender, but still holding their shape.

- Stir in the spinach, then cover and leave to stand for 5 minutes. Season to taste with salt and pepper before serving.

TOP TIP

You can also make this stew with veal instead of pork.

Lamb Chops with Apricots

ERVES 4

REPARATION TIME 15 MINUTES

OOKING TIME 2 HOURS

INGREDIENTS

tbsp olive oil

lamb chops

apricots, halved and stoned

cardamom pods

bay leaf

50 g / 5 ½ oz / 1 cup cherry tomatoes

)0 ml / 3 ½ fl. oz / ½ cup dry white wine

)0 ml / 7 fl. oz / 1 ⅔ cups tomato passata

tbsp sorrel leaves, shredded

alt and pepper

METHOD

- Heat the oil in a frying pan and season the lamb with salt and pepper. Sear the chops on both sides, then transfer to a slow cooker and add the rest of the ingredients apart from the sorrel.

- Cover and cook on high for 2 hours, then garnish with sorrel and serve.

TOP TIP
This recipe is also delicious made with peaches or plums.

Ham and Bean Soup

SERVES 6

PREPARATION TIME 5 MINUTES

COOKING TIME 6 HOURS

INGREDIENTS

225 g / 8 oz / 1 ½ cups piece boiling
   ham, diced
1 onion, finely chopped
1 celery stick, sliced
1 carrot, chopped
2 cloves of garlic, crushed
1 medium tomato, diced
300 g / 10 ½ oz / 2 cups haricot beans, soaked
   overnight and drained
1.2 litres / 2 pint / 5 cups vegetable stock
1 bay leaf
salt and pepper

METHOD

- Stir all of the ingredients together in a slow cooker, then cover and cook on medium for 6 hours.

- Taste the soup for seasoning and adjust with salt and pepper, then ladle into warm bowls and serve.

TOP TIP
Add a handful of fresh peas to the soup 10 minutes before the end of cooking.

Chicken, Potato and Pepper Tagine

SERVES 4

PREPARATION TIME 20 MINUTES

COOKING TIME 2 HOURS

INGREDIENTS

tbsp olive oil

chicken legs

onion, sliced

small potatoes, cut into wedges

red pepper, deseeded and diced

cloves of garlic, finely chopped

5 cm (1 in) piece fresh root ginger, finely chopped

tsp ground cumin

tsp ground coriander (cilantro)

tsp ground ginger

pinch of saffron

50 ml / 9 fl. oz / 1 cup chicken stock

ea salt

METHOD

- Preheat the oven to 160°C (140°C fan) / 325F / gas 3.

- Heat the oil in a large frying pan and season the chicken with salt. Sear the chicken legs on all sides, then transfer to a tagine.

- Mix with in the rest of the ingredients, then put on the lid and transfer the tagine to the oven.

- Cook the tagine for 2 hours, then leave to stand for 15 minutes before serving.

TOP TIP

Add a sliced chorizo to the tagine for a spicy kick.

Pot Roasted Chicken with Vegetables

SERVES 4

PREPARATION TIME 15 MINUTES

COOKING TIME 2 HOURS

INGREDIENTS

1 oven-ready chicken

2 tbsp olive oil

1 red onion, thickly sliced

2 celery sticks, chopped

1 yellow pepper, deseeded and cut
   into chunks

2 tbsp rosemary

100 g / 3 ½ oz / ⅔ cup kalamata olives

700 ml / 1 pint 3 ½ fl. oz / 2 ¾ cups dry white
   wine

salt and pepper

METHOD

- Preheat the oven to 180°C (160°C fan) / 350F / gas 4 and season the chicken all over with salt and pepper.

- Heat the oil in a frying pan and sear the chicken on all sides.

- Transfer the chicken to a large ovenproof saucepan or casserole dish and surround with the vegetables, rosemary and olives.

- Pour over the wine, then cover the pan and transfer to the oven. Roast for 1 hour 30 minutes, then remove the lid and return to the oven for a further 30 minutes.

TOP TIP

This method also works well with pheasant when in season.

Coq au Vin

SERVES 4

PREPARATION TIME 20 MINUTES

COOKING TIME 5 HOURS

INGREDIENTS

8 small chicken legs

3 tbsp plain (all purpose) flour

1 tsp mustard powder

3 tbsp olive oil

2 tbsp butter

150 g / 5 ½ oz / 1 cup pancetta, cubed

200 g / 7 oz / 1 ⅓ cups baby onions, peeled

a few sprigs of thyme

600 ml / 1 pint / 2 ½ cups red wine

150 g / 5 ½ oz / 2 cups button mushrooms, sliced

flat leaf parsley to garnish

salt and pepper

METHOD

- Season the chicken well with salt and pepper, then toss with the flour and mustard powder to coat.

- Heat half of the oil and butter in a sauté pan and sear the chicken pieces on all sides.

- Remove the chicken from the pan and add the rest of the oil and butter, followed by the pancetta, onions and thyme. Sauté for 5 minutes, then pour in the wine and bring to a simmer.

- Scrape the mixture into a slow cooker and add the seared chicken legs. Cover and cook on low for 4 hours, then stir in the mushrooms and cook for 1 more hour.

- Taste and adjust the seasoning with salt and pepper, then serve garnished with parsley.

TOP TIP

This recipe is also delicious made with guinea fowl or pheasant.

Pot-roasted Paupiettes of Veal

SERVES 4
PREPARATION TIME 25 MINUTES
COOKING TIME 1 HOUR

INGREDIENTS

4 good quality pork sausages, skinned

4 veal escalopes

2 tbsp olive oil

1 onion, sliced

2 carrots, sliced

a few sprigs of thyme

200 g / 7 oz / ¾ cup canned tomatoes, chopped

150 ml / 5 ½ fl. oz / ⅔ cup dry white wine

salt and pepper

METHOD

- Preheat the oven to 180°C (160°C fan) / 350F / gas 4.

- Put a quarter of the sausage meat on top of each escalope, then gather up the sides into a cushion shape and tie securely with string.

- Heat the oil in a frying pan and sear the paupiettes on all sides.

- Transfer the paupiettes to a cast iron casserole dish and surround with the onion, carrots and thyme. Stir the tomatoes into the wine, then pour it over the top.

- Cover the pan and cook in the oven for 1 hour. Season the vegetables to taste with salt and pepper just before serving.

TOP TIP

This recipe can also be made with turkey or pork escalopes.

Beef in Red Wine with Shallots

SERVES 4

PREPARATION TIME 20 MINUTES

COOKING TIME 6 HOURS

INGREDIENTS

500 g / 1 lb / 3 cups chuck steak, cut into large chunks

2 tbsp plain (all purpose) flour

2 tbsp olive oil

8 large shallots, halved

500 ml / 17 ½ fl. oz / 2 cups red wine

2 bay leaves

flat leaf parsley to garnish

mashed potato to serve

salt and pepper

METHOD

- Season the beef with salt and pepper and dust the pieces with flour to coat. Heat the oil in a large frying pan and sear the beef in batches on all sides. Remove the beef from the pan, then colour the cut side of the shallots.

- Transfer the beef and shallots to a slow cooker, tuck in the bay leaves and pour over the wine. Season well with salt and pepper.

- Put the lid on the slow cooker and cook on low for 6 hours, stirring every 2 hours. Garnish with parsley and serve with mashed potato.

TOP TIP

Try using white wine for a lighter stew.

Pot-roasted Rabbit

SERVES 4

PREPARATION TIME 15 MINUTES

COOKING TIME 1 HOUR

INGREDIENTS

1 rabbit, jointed

1 tbsp plain (all purpose) flour

2 tbsp olive oil

1 onion, sliced

2 carrots, sliced

1 tbsp sage leaves, chopped, plus extra to
   garnish

150 ml / 5 ½ fl. oz / ⅔ cup dry white wine

150 ml / 5 ½ fl. oz / ⅔ cup chicken stock

salt and pepper

METHOD

- Preheat the oven to 180°C (160°C
  fan) / 350F / gas 4.

- Season the rabbit well with salt and
  pepper, then dust with flour to coat.

- Heat the oil in a frying pan and sear
  the rabbit on all sides.

- Transfer the rabbit to a cast iron
  casserole dish and surround with
  the onion, carrots and sage. Stir the
  stock and wine together, then pour it
  over the top.

- Cover the pan and cook in the oven
  for 1 hour. Season to taste with salt
  and pepper, then serve, garnished
  with sage.

TOP TIP

Try replacing half of
the carrots with
parsnips.

Les Confitures Extra
de
Christine Ferber

Framboises et viole...

Preserves

Apple, Pear and Rhubarb Compote

SERVES 6

PREPARATION TIME 10 MINUTES

COOKING TIME 2 HOURS

INGREDIENTS

4 rhubarb stalks, chopped
2 Bramley apples, peeled, cored and diced
6 pears, peeled, cored and diced
6 tbsp caster (superfine) sugar

METHOD

- Mix all of the ingredients together in a slow cooker, then put on the lid and cook on low for 2 hours.

- Puree the compote with a liquidiser or mouli and serve warm or chilled.

TOP TIP

This makes a great accompaniment to grilled mackerel.

Blackberry and Raspberry Jam

MAKES 3 x 450 g JARS
PREPARATION TIME 5 MINUTES
COOKING TIME 4–5 HOURS

INGREDIENTS

500 g / 1 lb 2 oz / 3 ½ cups raspberries
500 g / 1 lb 2 oz / 3 ½ cups blackberries
900 g / 2 lb / 4 cups preserving sugar
50 g / 1 ¾ oz / ¼ cup powdered pectin
2 tbsp lemon juice

METHOD

- Stir all of the ingredients together in a large slow cooker.

- Cook on low for 2 hours, stirring well half way through.

- Put a saucer in the freezer. Increase the heat to high and cook for 2 hours. To test if the jam is ready, spoon a small amount onto the frozen saucer. Wait a few seconds, then push the side of the jam with a spoon. If the surface wrinkles, it is ready. If not, continue to cook on high and check again every 30 minutes.

- Ladle the hot jam into sterilised jars and screw the lids on securely.

TOP TIP
Try using the jam as the filling for a sponge cake.

Apricot, Almond and Pistachio Jam

MAKES 3 x 450 g JARS

PREPARATION TIME 5 MINUTES

COOKING TIME 4–5 HOURS

INGREDIENTS

1 kg / 2 lb 3 oz / 5 ½ cups apricots, quartered
 and stoned

900 g / 2 lb / 4 cups preserving sugar

50 g / 1 ¾ oz / ¼ cup powdered pectin

100 g / 2 ⅓ oz / 1 ⅓ cups flaked (slivered)
 almonds

100 g / 3 ½ oz / ¾ cup slivered pistachio nuts

METHOD

- Stir the apricots, sugar and pectin together in a large slow cooker.

- Cook on low for 2 hours, stirring well half way through.

- Put a saucer in the freezer. Increase the heat to high and cook for 2 hours. To test if the jam is ready, spoon a small amount onto the frozen saucer. Wait a few seconds, then push the side of the jam with a spoon. If the surface wrinkles, it is ready. If not, continue to cook on high and check again every 30 minutes.

- Stir the almonds and pistachio nuts into the jam, then ladle it into sterilised jars and screw the lids on securely.

TOP TIP
This jam makes a great filling for a bakewell tart.

PRESERVES

Strawberry Jam

MAKES 3 x 450 g JARS
PREPARATION TIME 5 MINUTES
COOKING TIME 4–5 HOURS

INGREDIENTS

1 kg / 2 lb 3 oz / 7 cups strawberries, sliced
900 g / 2 lb / 4 cups preserving sugar
50 g / 1 ¾ oz / ¼ cup powdered pectin
2 lemons, juiced

METHOD

- Stir all of the ingredients together in a large slow cooker.

- Cook on low for 2 hours, stirring well half way through.

- Put a saucer in the freezer. Increase the heat to high and cook for 2 hours. To test if the jam is ready, spoon a small amount onto the frozen saucer. Wait a few seconds, then push the side of the jam with a spoon. If the surface wrinkles, it is ready. If not, continue to cook on high and check again every 30 minutes.

- Ladle the hot jam into sterilised jars and screw the lids on securely.

TOP TIP
Try adding the seeds from two vanilla pods just before decanting into jars.

Slow-baked Apricots

SERVES 4

PREPARATION TIME 5 MINUTES

COOKING TIME 1 HOUR 30 MINUTES

INGREDIENTS

20 apricots, halved and stoned

50 g / 1 ¾ oz / ¼ cup caster (superfine) sugar

250 ml / 9 fl. oz / 1 cup white grape juice

3 tbsp apricot brandy

2 tbsp butter, melted

METHOD

- Preheat the oven to 150°C (130°C fan) / 300F / gas 2.

- Stir all of the ingredients together in a cast iron casserole dish. Put a lid on the dish then bake for 1 hour 30 minutes, stirring half way through.

TOP TIP
Serve the apricots hot with cold vanilla ice cream.

Les Confitures Extra .
de
Christine Ferber
Framboises et viole*

Raspberry and Violet Conserve

MAKES 4 x 450 g JARS

PREPARATION TIME 5 MINUTES

COOKING TIME 4–5 HOURS

INGREDIENTS

2 kg / 4 lb 6 oz / 14 cups raspberries

900 g / 2 lb / 4 cups preserving sugar

50 g / 1 ¾ oz / ¼ cup powdered pectin

75 ml / 2 ½ fl. oz / ⅓ cup violet syrup

METHOD

- Stir the raspberries, sugar and pectin together in a large slow cooker.

- Cook on low for 2 hours, stirring well half way through. Pass the mixture through a sieve to remove the seeds and wash and dry the slow cooker.

- Put a saucer in the freezer. Return the puree to the slow cooker, then increase the heat to high and cook for 2 hours. To test if the confiture is ready, spoon a small amount onto the frozen saucer. If it is just thick enough to spread, it is ready. If it is too runny, continue to cook on high and check again every 30 minutes.

- When you are happy with the consistency, stir in the violet syrup then ladle the hot conserve into sterilised jars and screw the lids on securely. The high fruit content of this conserve means it should be stored in the fridge and has a shorter shelf life than other jams.

TOP TIP

Try using stoned dates in place of the figs.

Lemon and Lime Marmalade

MAKES 3 x 450 g JARS

PREPARATION TIME 15 MINUTES

COOKING TIME 6–7 HOURS

INGREDIENTS

2 unwaxed lemons, quartered and
    pips removed

4 unwaxed limes, quartered

900 g / 2 lb / 4 cups preserving sugar

METHOD

- Put the lemons and limes into a slow cooker and pour in 1.2 litres of water. Cook on low for 4 hours.

- Transfer the contents of the slow cooker to a liquidiser and pulse until the fruit is finely chopped. Return the pulp to the pan and stir in the sugar until dissolved.

- Put a saucer in the freezer. Increase the heat to high and cook for 2 hours. To test if the marmalade is ready, spoon a small amount onto the frozen saucer. Wait a few seconds, then push the side of the marmalade with a spoon. If the surface wrinkles, it is ready. If not, continue to cook on high and check again every 30 minutes.

- Ladle the hot marmalade into sterilised jars and screw the lids on securely.

TOP TIP

Try using the marmalade as an usual filling for a Victoria sponge.

Raspberry Jam

AKES 3 x 450 g JARS
REPARATION TIME 5 MINUTES
OKING TIME 4–5 HOURS

GREDIENTS

kg / 2 lb 3 oz / 7 cups raspberries
0 g / 2 lb / 4 cups preserving sugar
g / 1 ¾ oz / ¼ cup powdered pectin
bsp lemon juice

METHOD

- Stir all of the ingredients together in a large slow cooker.

- Cook on low for 2 hours, stirring well half way through.

- Put a saucer in the freezer. Increase the heat to high and cook for 2 hours. To test if the jam is ready, spoon a small amount onto the frozen saucer. Wait a few seconds, then push the side of the jam with a spoon. If the surface wrinkles, it is ready. If not, continue to cook on high and check again every 30 minutes.

- Ladle the hot jam into sterilised jars and screw the lids on securely.

TOP TIP
Serve the jam with fresh scones and clotted cream.

Exotic Fruit Compote

SERVES 6
PREPARATION TIME 10 MINUTES
COOKING TIME 1 HOUR 30 MINUTES

INGREDIENTS

3 mangoes, peeled, stoned and diced
2 papayas, peeled, deseeded and diced
6 passion fruit, halved
2 limes, juiced
4 tbsp caster (superfine) sugar
2 tbsp coconut rum

METHOD

- Put the mango and papaya in a slow cooker and scoop in the passion fruit seeds and flesh. Stir in the lime juice, sugar and coconut rum.

- Put on the lid and cook on low for 1 hour 30 minutes or until the fruit has started to break down. Leave the compote chunky or use a stick blender to purée the fruit and serve hot or chilled.

TOP TIP
Try serving the compote with coconut ice cream.

Apple
Compote

SERVES 6

PREPARATION TIME 5 MINUTES

COOKING TIME 2 HOURS

INGREDIENTS

Bramley apples, peeled, cored and diced

eating apples, peeled, cored and diced

lemon, juiced

150 ml / 5 ½ fl. oz / ⅔ cup apple juice

tbsp caster (superfine) sugar

METHOD

- Mix all of the ingredients together in a slow cooker, then put on the lid and cook on low for 2 hours.

- Puree the compote with a liquidiser or mouli and serve warm or chilled.

TOP TIP

This compote makes a delicious accompaniment to roast pork or duck.

143

Fig and Pine Nut Conserve

MAKES 4 x 450 g JARS

PREPARATION TIME 5 MINUTES

COOKING TIME 4–5 HOURS

INGREDIENTS

2 kg / 4 lb 6 oz / 10 cups ripe figs, diced
2 lemons, juiced
900 g / 2 lb / 4 cups preserving sugar
50 g / 1 ¾ oz / ¼ cup powdered pectin
150 g / 5 ½ oz / 1 cup pine nuts

METHOD

- Stir the figs, lemon juice, sugar and pectin together in a large slow cooker.

- Cook on low for 2 hours, stirring well half way through. Use a mouli or food processor to puree the fruit and wash and dry the slow cooker.

- Put a saucer in the freezer. Return the puree to the slow cooker, then increase the heat to high and cook for 2 hours. To test if the conserve is ready, spoon a small amount onto the frozen saucer. If it is just thick enough to spread, it is ready. If it is too runny, continue to cook on high and check again every 30 minutes.

- When you are happy with the consistency, stir in the pine nuts then ladle the hot confiture into sterilised jars and screw the lids on securely. The high fruit content of this conserve means it should be stored in the fridge and has a shorter shelf life than other jams.

TOP TIP
Serve the confiture with mature cheeses.

Peach Jam

MAKES 3 x 450 g JARS

PREPARATION TIME 5 MINUTES

COOKING TIME 4–5 HOURS

INGREDIENTS

1 kg / 2 lb 3 oz / 5 ½ cups peaches stoned
  and chopped

900 g / 2 lb / 4 cups preserving sugar

50 g / 1 ¾ oz / ¼ cup powdered pectin

METHOD

- Stir the peaches, sugar and pectin together in a large slow cooker.

- Cook on low for 2 hours, stirring well half way through.

- Put a saucer in the freezer. Increase the heat to high and cook for 2 hours. To test if the jam is ready, spoon a small amount onto the frozen saucer. Wait a few seconds, then push the side of the jam with a spoon. If the surface wrinkles, it is ready. If not, continue to cook on high and check again every 30 minutes.

- Ladle the hot jam into sterilised jars and screw the lids on securely.

TOP TIP
This jam is delicious served with fresh crepes and vanilla ice cream.

Apple and Raspberry Compote

SERVES 6

PREPARATION TIME 5 MINUTES

COOKING TIME 2 HOURS

INGREDIENTS

2 Bramley apples, peeled, cored and diced
6 eating apples, peeled, cored and diced
200 g / 7 oz / 1 ⅓ cups raspberries
150 ml / 5 ½ fl. oz / ⅔ cup apple juice
4 tbsp caster (superfine) sugar

METHOD

- Mix all of the ingredients together in a slow cooker, then put on the lid and cook on low for 2 hours.

- Pass the compote through a mouli or sieve to purée the apples and remove the raspberry seeds. Taste the compote and add a little more sugar if it is too sharp.

TOP TIP
Serve the compote for breakfast with thick Greek yoghurt and granola.

Pear Compote

SERVES 6

PREPARATION TIME 5 MINUTES

COOKING TIME 2 HOURS

INGREDIENTS

Bramley apples, peeled, cored and diced

pears, peeled, cored and diced

lemons, juiced

tbsp caster (superfine) sugar

METHOD

- Mix all of the ingredients together in a slow cooker, then put on the lid and cook on low for 2 hours.

- Puree the compote with a liquidiser or mouli and serve warm or chilled.

TOP TIP

This compote makes a delicious accompaniment to roast game dishes.

Cranberry Sauce

MAKES 1 x 450 g JAR

PREPARATION TIME 10 MINUTES

COOKING TIME 2 HOURS

INGREDIENTS

450 g / 1 lb / 2 ½ cups cranberries

200 g / 7 oz / ¾ cup caster (superfine) sugar

1 orange, juiced

METHOD

- Stir the cranberries, sugar and orange juice together in a small slow cooker.

- Cover and cook on high for 2 hours or until the cranberries have burst and softened.

- Ladle the sauce into a sterilised jar and leave to cool completely before storing in the fridge.

TOP TIP

A finely choppped red chilli (chili) for a spicy kick.

PRESERVES

Cinnamon Apple Compote

MAKES 2 x 450 g JARS

PREPARATION TIME 5 MINUTES

COOKING TIME 2 HOURS

INGREDIENTS

Bramley apples, peeled, cored and diced

eating apples, peeled, cored and diced

lemon, juiced

50 ml / 5 ½ fl. oz / ⅔ cup apple juice

tbsp caster (superfine) sugar

cinnamon sticks

METHOD

- Mix all of the ingredients together in a slow cooker, then put on the lid and cook on low for 2 hours.

- Spoon the compote into sterilised jars and seal whilst still hot.

TOP TIP

Use the compote as the filling to mini apple pies.

Poached Rhubarb in Chocolate Cases

SERVES 6

PREPARATION TIME 45 MINUTES

COOKING TIME 2 HOURS

INGREDIENTS

800 g / 1 lb 12 ½ oz / 5 cups rhubarb stalks

150 g / 5 ½ oz / ⅔ cup caster (superfine) sugar

50 g / 1 ¾ oz / ⅓ cup white chocolate

150 g / 5 ½ oz / 1 cup milk chocolate

METHOD

- Cut the rhubarb into short lengths and put it in a slow cooker. Sprinkle over the sugar and 3 tbsp of water, then cover and cook on medium for 2 hours. Leave to cool, then chill in the fridge.

- To make the chocolate cases, line 6 tartlet cases with cling film. Melt the white chocolate in a microwave or bain marie, then drizzle it into the cases. Chill in the fridge for 15 minutes to set.

- Melt the milk chocolate, then spoon it into the tartlet cases and tilt to coat in a thin, even layer. Turn the moulds upside down onto a tray and return to the fridge for 20 minutes.

- Unmould the chocolate cases and remove the cling film, then spoon in the rhubarb compote to serve.

TOP TIP

Try serving the desserts with stem ginger ice cream.

Spiced Plum Compote

SERVES 6
PREPARATION TIME 5 MINUTES
COOKING TIME 2 HOURS

INGREDIENTS

star anise
cinnamon stick, broken into pieces
cloves
6 plums, peeled, stoned and chopped
tbsp caster (superfine) sugar

METHOD

- Put the spices in a small square of muslin and tie into a bag with string. Put the spice bag in a slow cooker with the plums and sugar and drizzle over 3 tbsp of water.

- Cover and cook on medium for 2 hours. Taste for sweetness and add extra sugar if necessary. Discard the spice bag and serve warm or cold.

TOP TIP
Try serving this compote with fresh crepes and vanilla ice cream.

Desserts

Chocolate Rice Pudding

SERVES 4

PREPARATION TIME 15 MINUTES

COOKING TIME 3 HOURS

INGREDIENTS

50 g / 1 ¾ oz / ¼ cup butter, plus extra
for greasing
1.2 litres / 2 pints / 4 ½ cups whole milk
3 tbsp unsweetened cocoa powder
110 g / 4 oz / ½ cup short-grain rice
75 g / 2 ½ oz / ⅓ cup caster (superfine) sugar
100 g / 3 ½ oz / ⅔ cup dark chocolate
(minimum 70% cocoa solids)
4 tbsp clotted cream

METHOD

- Butter the inside of a slow cooker.
  Stir all of the ingredients together
  except for the chocolate and cream,
  then tip the mixture into the
  slow cooker.

- Cover and cook on high for 3 hours,
  stirring once every hour.

- Break the chocolate into small
  squares. Remove the inner pan from
  the slow cooker and distribute the
  chocolate over the surface of the rice
  pudding. Cover and leave to stand for
  5 minutes, then gently stir everything
  together until homogenised.

- Serve warm or chilled, topped with a
  spoonful of clotted cream.

TOP TIP
Add zest of an orange
and a pinch of Cayenne
pepper before
cooking.

Chocolate Fondue

RVES 6–8
REPARATION TIME 5 MINUTES
COKING TIME 30 MINUTES

GREDIENTS

0 g / 7 oz / 1 ⅓ cups dark chocolate
(minimum 70% cocoa solids)
0 ml / 10 ½ fl. oz / 1 ¼ cups double (heavy)
cream
bsp butter
bsp runny honey
bsp brandy
all sponge cakes to serve

METHOD

- Break the chocolate into small squares and mix it with the cream, butter, honey and brandy in a small slow cooker. Cover and cook on low for 30 minutes or until the chocolate has melted and homogenised with the cream, stirring every 10 minutes.

- Serve the fondue in the slow cooker at the table to keep it warm or transfer to a serving bowl. Thread small sponge cakes onto skewers for your guests to dip in.

TOP TIP
Add the grated zest of an orange and a pinch of Cayenne pepper for added zing.

Pears in Red Wine with Thyme

SERVES 4

PREPARATION TIME 5 MINUTES

COOKING TIME 2 HOURS

INGREDIENTS

8 small pears, peeled and cored, stalks
  left intact
2 tbsp caster (superfine) sugar
500 ml / 17 ½ fl. oz / 2 cups red wine
3 sprigs of thyme

METHOD

- Put everything in a slow cooker,
  then cover and cook on medium
  for 2 hours, turning the pears half
  way through.

- Serve warm or chilled.

TOP TIP
You could also use rosemary instead of thyme.

Orange and Ginger Bundt Cake

SERVES 8
PREPARATION TIME 15 MINUTES
COOKING TIME 3 HOURS

INGREDIENTS

225 g / 8 oz / 1 ½ cups self-raising flour
100 g / 3 ½ oz / ½ cup butter, cubed
100 g / 3 ½ oz / ½ cup caster (superfine) sugar
1 tsp ground ginger
1 large egg
75 ml / 2 ½ fl. oz / ⅓ cup whole milk
1 orange, juiced and zest finely grated

METHOD

- Put a rack in the bottom of a slow cooker and add 2.5 cm (1 in) of boiling water. Butter a bundt tin that will fit inside your slow cooker.

- Sieve the flour into a mixing bowl and rub in the butter until it resembles fine breadcrumbs then stir in the sugar and ground ginger.

- Lightly beat the egg with the milk, orange juice and zest and stir it into the dry ingredients until just combined.

- Scrape the mixture into the tin then transfer it to the slow cooker. Cook on high for 3 hours or until a skewer inserted in the centre comes out clean. Transfer the cake to a wire rack and leave to cool completely.

TOP TIP
Drizzle the cake with melted dark chocolate and sprinkle with crystalised ginger pieces.

Chunky Pear and Vanilla Compote

SERVES 6
PREPARATION TIME 5 MINUTES
COOKING TIME 2 HOURS

INGREDIENTS

2 Bramley apples, peeled, cored and diced
8 pears, peeled, cored and diced
1 lemon, juiced
4 tbsp caster (superfine) sugar
1 vanilla pod, split lengthways
vanilla ice cream to serve

METHOD

- Mix all of the ingredients together, apart from the ice cream, in a slow cooker, then put on the lid and cook on low for 2 hours.

- Leave the compote to cool to room temperature, then chill in the fridge. Serve with scoops of vanilla ice cream.

TOP TIP
Use the compote as a base for crumbles or pies.

Poached Peaches with Lavender

SERVES 4

PREPARATION TIME 30 MINUTES

COOKING TIME 1 HOUR 30 MINUTES

INGREDIENTS

peaches, halved and stoned

100 g / 3 ½ oz / ½ cup caster (superfine) sugar

sprigs lavender

METHOD

- Put the peaches in a slow cooker with the sugar and lavender and pour over 200 ml / 7 fl. oz / ¾ cup of water.

- Cover and cook on medium for 1 hour 30 minutes or until the fruit is tender, but still holding its shape.

- Peel off and discard the peach skins and lavender stems before serving.

TOP TIP
This recipe also works really well with plums.

Vanilla Poached Cherries

SERVES 6

PREPARATION TIME 10 MINUTES

COOKING TIME 1 HOUR 30 MINUTES

INGREDIENTS

900 g / 2 lb / 5 cups black cherries, stoned

100 g / 3 ½ oz / ½ cup caster (superfine) sugar

100 ml / 3 ½ fl. oz / ½ cup rosé wine

1 vanilla pod, split lengthways

3 tbsp kirsch

vanilla ice cream to serve

METHOD

- Mix the cherries with the sugar, wine and vanilla pod in a slow cooker. Cover and cook on medium for 1 hour 30 minutes then stir in the kirsch and leave to cool.

- Discard the vanilla pod, then spoon the cherries and their cooking liquor into bowls and serve with vanilla ice cream.

TOP TIP

You can also use mirabelles or small greengages in place of the cherries.

Chocolate Muffin Puddings

MAKES 6
PREPARATION TIME 20 MINUTES
COOKING TIME 2 HOURS

INGREDIENTS

1 large egg
125 ml / 4 ½ fl. oz / ½ cup sunflower oil
125 ml / 4 ½ fl. oz / ½ cup milk
350 g / 12 ½ oz / 2 ⅓ cups self-raising flour, sifted
50 g / 1 ¾ oz / ½ cup unsweetened cocoa powder, sifted
1 tsp baking powder
200 g / 7 oz / ¾ cup caster (superfine) sugar
6 sugar cubes

METHOD

- Put a rack inside a slow cooker and add 2.5 cm (1 in) of boiling water, then set it to high. Butter 6 mini casserole dishes or pudding basins.

- Beat the egg in a jug with the oil and milk until well mixed. Mix the flour, cocoa, baking powder and caster sugar in a bowl, then pour in the egg mixture and stir just enough to combine.

- Divide the mixture between the dishes and transfer to the slow cooker. Lay 3 layers of kitchen paper over the top of the slow cooker before putting on the lid to absorb the condensing steam.

- Cook the puddings on high for 2 hours. Crumble over the sugar cubes and serve warm.

TOP TIP

Add the grated zest of an orange and a pinch of Cayenne pepper for added zing.

Blueberry and Raspberry Bread and Butter Pudding

SERVES 4–6

PREPARATION TIME 20 MINUTES

COOKING TIME 1 HOUR 30 MINUTES

INGREDIENTS

8 slices white bread

4 tbsp butter, softened

100 g / 3 ½ oz / ⅔ cup blueberries

50 g / 1 ¾ oz / ⅓ cup raspberries

250 ml / 9 fl. oz / 1 cup milk

200 ml / 7 fl. oz / ¾ cup double (heavy) cream

4 large egg yolks

75 g / 2 ½ oz / ⅓ cup caster (superfine) sugar

1 lemon, zest finely grated

demerara sugar for sprinkling

METHOD

- Spread the bread with butter then cut each slice into squares and toss with the blueberries and raspberries in a baking dish.

- Whisk the milk, cream, eggs, sugar and lemon zest together and pour it over the bread, then leave to soak for 10 minutes.

- Preheat the oven to 150°C (130°C fan) / 300F / gas 2. Bake the pudding for 1 hour 30 minutes or until the custard is just set with a slight wobble in the centre.

- Sprinkle with demerara sugar before serving.

TOP TIP
You can also use stoned cherries instead of the blueberries and raspberries.

Chocolate and Cherry Summer Pudding

SERVES 8

PREPARATION TIME 45 MINUTES

COOKING TIME 2 HOURS

CHILLING TIME 4 HOURS

INGREDIENTS

450 g / 1 lb / 3 cups cherries, stoned and
    halved

4 tbsp caster (superfine) sugar

4 tbsp kirsch

5 slices white bread, crusts removed

250 ml / 9 fl. oz / 1 cup double (heavy) cream

250 g / 9 oz / 1 ⅔ cups dark chocolate
    (minimum 60 % cocoa solids), chopped

METHOD

- Stir the cherries, sugar and kirsch together in a small slow cooker. Cover and cook on low for 2 hours, stirring half way through. Leave to cool, then strain the cherries through a sieve and collect the juice.

- Line a pudding basin with cling film. Dip the bread in the cherry juice and use it to line the pudding basin, saving one slice for the lid.

- Bring the cream to a simmer then pour it over the chocolate and stir gently to emulsify. Fold the cherries into the chocolate ganache and spoon it into the pudding basin. Top with the last slice of soaked bread then cover the basin with cling film.

- Put a small board on top of the pudding basin and weigh it down with a can, then leave it to chill in the fridge for at least 4 hours.

- When you're ready to serve, invert the pudding onto a plate and peel away the cling film.

TOP TIP
Serve the pudding with clotted cream for an extra touch of luxury.

Apple Cake

SERVES 6

PREPARATION TIME 15 MINUTES

COOKING TIME 2–3 HOURS

INGREDIENTS

200 g / 7 oz / ¾ cup caster (superfine) sugar

1 large egg

3 tablespoons sunflower oil

1 tsp vanilla extract

150 g / 5 ½ oz / 1 cup plain (all purpose) flour

½ tsp bicarbonate of (baking) soda

½ tsp baking powder

½ tsp ground cinnamon

3 apples, peeled, cored and sliced

METHOD

- Whisk the sugar, egg, oil and vanilla extract together with an electric whisk for 4 minutes or until thick. Stir the flour, raising agents and cinnamon together, then fold in the egg mixture and apples.

- Butter the inside of a small slow cooker and scrape in the cake mixture. Put the lid on and bake on medium for 2 hours.

- Test the cake by inserting a skewer into the centre – if it comes out clean, the cake is down. Otherwise, continue to cook and check again every 30 minutes until it is ready.

- Leave to cool completely before cutting and serving.

TOP TIP
Try using pears instead of apples and add a handful of sultanas.

ndividual Bread and Butter Puddings

AKES 4

REPARATION TIME 20 MINUTES

OOKING TIME 1 HOUR

NGREDIENTS

thick slices white bread

tbsp butter, softened

tbsp sultanas

50 ml / 9 fl. oz / 1 cup milk

00 ml / 7 fl. oz / ¾ cup double (heavy) cream

large egg yolks

5 g / 2 ½ oz / ⅓ cup caster (superfine) sugar

lemon, zest finely grated

utmeg to grate

METHOD

- Spread the bread with butter and cut each piece into 4 triangles. Butter 4 small baking dishes and layer up the bread inside with the sultanas.

- Whisk the milk, cream, eggs, sugar and lemon zest together and divide it between the dishes, then leave to soak for 10 minutes.

- Preheat the oven to 150°C (130°C fan) / 300F / gas 2. Bake the puddings for 1 hour or until the custard is just set with a slight wobble. Grate over a little nutmeg and serve hot or cold.

TOP TIP

Spread the bread with marmalade and use chocolate chips instead of raisins.

Fig and Apple Crumble

SERVES 4

PREPARATION TIME 15 MINUTES

COOKING TIME 1 HOUR 30 MINUTES

INGREDIENTS

4 eating apples, peeled, cored and diced

4 figs, cut into quarters

2 tbsp caster (superfine) sugar

75 g / 2 ½ oz / ⅓ cup butter

50 g / 1 ¾ oz / ⅓ cup plain (all purpose) flour

25 g / 1 oz / ¼ cup ground almonds

40 g / 1 ½ oz / ¼ cup light brown sugar

50 g / 1 ¾ oz / ½ cup porridge oats

METHOD

- Preheat the oven to 160°C (140°C fan) / 325F / gas 3.

- Mix the apples with the figs and caster sugar in a baking dish. Cover the dish with foil and bake in the oven for 1 hour.

- Take the fruit out of the oven and increase the temperature to 180°C (160°C fan) / 350F / gas 4.

- Rub the butter into the flour and stir in the ground almonds, sugar and oats. Take a handful of the topping and squeeze it into a clump, then crumble it over the fruit. Repeat with the rest of the crumble mixture then bake for 30 minutes or until the topping is golden brown.

TOP TIP

Try using stoned dates in place of the figs.

Crème Caramel

MAKES 6

PREPARATION TIME 30 MINUTES

COOKING TIME 3 HOURS

CHILLING TIME 4 HOURS

INGREDIENTS

175 g / 6 oz / ¾ cup caster (superfine) sugar

2 tbsp butter, softened

600 ml / 1 pint / 2 ½ cups whole milk

4 large eggs

1 tsp vanilla bean paste

METHOD

- Preheat the slow cooker to low.

- Put 150 g / 5 oz / ⅔ cup of the sugar in a heavy-based saucepan and heat gently until it starts to turn liquid at the edges. Continue to heat and swirl the pan until the sugar has all melted and turned golden brown. Divide the caramel between 6 ramekin dishes and leave to set, then butter the sides of the ramekins.

- Whisk the milk, eggs and vanilla bean paste with the remaining sugar and divide between the ramekins. Cover each ramekin with buttered foil. Sit the ramekins in the slow cooker and pour enough boiling water around them to come halfway up the sides.

- Cook on low for 3 hours or until the crème caramels are just set with a slight wobble in the centre. Remove the ramekins from the slow cooker and chill for 4 hours or overnight.

- Give the ramekins a vigorous shake to loosen the crème caramels, then turn each one out onto a plate.

TOP TIP
Try flavouring the custard with lemon zest instead of vanilla.

Sweet Apricot Tagine

SERVES 2

PREPARATION TIME 10 MINUTES

COOKING TIME 1 HOUR

INGREDIENTS

10 apricots
4 tbsp honey
½ tsp almond extract
½ tsp orange flower water
100 ml / 3 ½ fl. oz / ½ cup apple juice
2 tbsp flaked (slivered) almonds

METHOD

- Preheat the oven to 150°C (130°C fan) / 300F / gas 2.

- Arrange the apricots in 2 individual tagines. Stir the honey, almond extract and orange flower water into the apple juice, then spoon it over the apricots.

- Put the lids on the tagines and transfer them to the oven. Bake for 1 hour or until the apricots are tender through to the stones. Sprinkle with almonds and serve immediately.

TOP TIP
This recipe is also delicious made with peaches.

Pecan and Maple Syrup Cheesecake

RVES 8

EPARATION TIME 30 MINUTES

OKING TIME 3 HOURS

ILLING TIME 2 HOURS

GREDIENTS

0 g / 7 oz / ¾ cups digestive biscuits, crushed

g / 1 ¾ oz / ¼ cup butter, melted

0 g / 1 lb 5 oz / 2 ¾ cups cream cheese

0 ml / 5 fl. oz / ⅔ cup soured cream

arge eggs, plus 1 egg yolk

bsp plain (all purpose) flour

0 ml / 3 ½ fl. oz / ⅓ cup maple syrup

g / 2 ½ oz / ⅓ cup caster (superfine) sugar

R THE PECAN TOPPING

bsp maple syrup

g / 2 ½ oz / ⅔ cup pecan nuts, roughly chopped

METHOD

- Mix the biscuit crumbs with the butter and press into an even layer in the bottom of a spring-form cake tin that will fit inside your slow cooker.

- Whisk together the cream cheese, soured cream, eggs, egg yolk and flour until smooth. Divide the mixture between 2 bowls and beat the maple syrup into one half. Pour it into the tin and level the surface. Beat the caster sugar into the second bowl, then spoon it into the tin and level the surface.

- Put a rack into the bottom of your slow cooker and add 2.5 cm (1 in) of boiling water, then position the cake tin on top. Cover the top of the slow cooker with 3 layers of kitchen paper before putting on the lid. The paper will collect the condensed steam and stop it from dripping onto the cheesecake.

- Cook on high for 2 hours, then turn off the slow cooker and leave to cook in the residual heat without lifting the lid for 1 hour.

- Take the cheesecake out of the slow cooker and leave to cool to room temperature before chilling for at least 2 hours. Stir the maple syrup and pecans together and drizzle over the cheesecake before serving.

TOP TIP

If you can't find pecan nuts, use walnuts instead.

Orange Crème Caramel

SERVES 6

PREPARATION TIME 20 MINUTES

COOKING TIME 3 HOUR

CHILLING TIME 4 HOUR

INGREDIENTS

175 g / 6 oz / ¾ cup caster (superfine) sugar

1 tbsp butter, softened

500 ml / 17 ½ fl. oz / 2 cups whole milk

100 ml / 3 ½ fl. oz / ½ cup orange juice, sieved

4 large eggs

1 tsp orange zest, finely grated

1 tbsp Cointreau

METHOD

- Preheat the slow cooker to low.

- Put 150 g / 5 oz / ⅔ cup of the sugar in a heavy-based saucepan and heat gently until it starts to turn liquid at the edges. Continue to heat and swirl the pan until the sugar has all melted and turned golden brown. Divide the caramel between 6 ramekin dishes and leave to set, then butter the sides of the ramekins.

- Whisk the rest of the ingredients with the remaining of sugar and divide between the ramekins. Cover each ramekin with buttered foil. Sit the ramekins in the slow cooker and pour enough boiling water around them to come halfway up the sides.

- Cook on low for 3 hours or until the crème caramels are just set with a slight wobble in the centre. Remove the ramekins from the slow cooker and chill for 4 hours or overnight.

- Give the ramekins a vigorous shake to loosen the crème caramels, then turn each one out onto a plate.

TOP TIP
Try adding a pinch of Cayenne pepper to the custard for a spicy kick.

Stewed Cherries with Fromage Frais

METHOD

- Stir the cherries and caster sugar into the wine in a small slow cooker. Cover and cook on medium for 1 hour 30 minutes or until the cherries are starting to collapse. Stir in the kirsch and almond essence and leave to cool.

- Beat the fromage frais with the icing sugar until smooth then divide between 4 serving bowls or glasses.

- Spoon the stewed cherries over the top and serve immediately.

ERVES 4

PREPARATION TIME 10 MINUTES

COOKING TIME 1 HOUR 30 MINUTES

INGREDIENTS

50 g / 1 lb / 2 ½ cups cherries, stoned

00 g / 3 ½ oz / ½ cup caster (superfine) sugar

00 ml / 3 ½ fl. oz / ½ cup rosé wine

tbsp kirsch

½ tsp almond essence

50 g / 1 lb / 2 cups natural fromage frais

5 g / 2 ½ oz / ¾ cup icing (confectioners') sugar

TOP TIP

Spice up the cherries with a whole star anise while they're poaching.

Peach and Pomegranate Tagine

SERVES 2

PREPARATION TIME 10 MINUTES

COOKING TIME 45 MINUTES

INGREDIENTS

3 peaches, quartered and stoned

2 tbsp honey

1 tsp rose water

100 ml / 3 ½ fl. oz / ½ cup pomegranate juice

½ pomegranate

METHOD

- Preheat the oven to 150°C (130°C fan) / 300F / gas 2.

- Arrange the peach quarters in 2 individual tagines. Stir the honey and rose water into the pomegranate juice, then spoon it over the peaches.

- Put the lids on the tagines and transfer them to the oven. Bake for 45 minutes or until the peaches are tender.

- Hold the pomegranate over a bowl and hit the rounded side with a wooden spoon to release the seeds. Sprinkle the seeds over the peaches and serve immediately.

TOP TIP

Try adding a few chopped stoned dates to the tagine.

DESSERTS

Peach Compote with Poached Meringue

SERVES 6
PREPARATION TIME 20 MINUTES
COOKING TIME 1 HOUR 30 MINUTES

INGREDIENTS

12 ripe peaches, peeled, stoned and chopped
1 lemon, juiced
4 tbsp caster (superfine) sugar
2 tbsp brandy

FOR THE POACHED MERINGUE

600 ml / 1 pint / 2 ½ cups milk
4 large egg whites
110 g / 4 oz / ½ cup caster (superfine) sugar
2 tbsp toasted flaked (slivered) almonds

METHOD

- Toss the peaches with the lemon juice, sugar and brandy in a slow cooker. Put on the lid and cook on low for 1 hour 30 minutes or until the fruit has started to break down. Leave the compote chunky or use a stick blender to purée the fruit.

- Put the milk in a saucepan with 500 ml / 17 fl. oz / 2 cups of boiling water and bring to a gentle simmer.

- Whisk the egg whites until stiff, then gradually add the sugar, whisking until the mixture is thick and shiny.

- Transfer 6 heaped tablespoons of the mixture to the simmering milk and poach the meringues for 10 minutes, turning halfway through. Transfer the meringues to a wire rack and leave to steam dry for a few minutes.

- Serve the compote hot or chilled and top with the meringues and a sprinkle of almonds.

TOP TIP
This compote is also delicious made with apricots.

Poached Fruit with Raclette Crumble Topping

SERVES 4-6

PREPARATION TIME 30 MINUTES

COOKING TIME 1 HOUR 30 MINUTES

INGREDIENTS

2 eating apples, cored and cut into wedges
2 pears, peeled, cored and cut into wedges
1 peach, peeled, stoned and cut into wedges
500 ml / 17 ½ fl. oz / 2 cups apple juice
75 g / 2 ½ oz / ⅓ cup butter
50 g / 1 ¾ oz / ⅓ cup plain (all purpose) flour
25 g / 1 oz / ½ cup ground almonds
40 g / 1 ½ oz / ¼ cup light brown sugar

METHOD

- Put the fruit in a slow cooker and pour over the juice. Cook on medium for 1 hour 30 minutes or until the fruit is tender, but still holding its shape.

- Rub the butter into the flour and stir in the ground almonds and sugar, then transfer the mixture to a serving bowl.

- Set a raclette grill in the middle of the table and put it on to heat. Each diner can then put a few pieces of fruit in a raclette tray and sprinkle with the crumble topping before cooking it under the raclette grill.

TOP TIP
If you don't have a raclette, toast the crumble under a hot grill.

Pear, Orange and Cinnamon Tagine

SERVES 4

PREPARATION TIME 10 MINUTES

COOKING TIME 2 HOURS

INGREDIENTS

- pears, peeled, cored and quartered
- oranges
- tbsp honey
- cinnamon stick

METHOD

- Preheat the oven to 150°C (130°C fan) / 300F / gas 2.

- Arrange the pear quarters in 4 individual tagines. Cut 4 slices from one of the oranges and tuck a slice into each tagine, then squeeze over the juice from the remaining oranges and drizzle with honey. Break the cinnamon stick into shards and sprinkle a little into each tagine.

- Put the lids on the tagines and transfer them to the oven. Bake for 2 hour or until the pears are really tender.

TOP TIP

Try adding a few slices of fresh root ginger for a spicy kick.

Poached Apples with Sesame Caramel

SERVES 4

PREPARATION TIME 30 MINUTES

COOKING TIME 1 HOUR 30 MINUTES

INGREDIENTS

4 apples, peeled, cored and halved
500 ml / 17 ½ fl. oz / 2 cups apple juice
1 tbsp butter
1 tsp sesame oil
½ tbsp sesame seeds

METHOD

- Arrange the apples cut side down in a single layer in a slow cooker. Pour over the apple juice then cook on medium for 1 hour 30 minutes or until the apples are tender to the point of a knife.

- Drain the apples through a colander and collect the juice in a saucepan. Boil the juice over a high heat until it has reduced to a syrupy consistency, then whisk in the butter and sesame oil to make a shiny caramel sauce.

- Divide the apples between 4 bowls, then drizzle over the sauce and sprinkle with sesame seeds.

TOP TIP
Serve the apples warm with cold vanilla ice cream.

Strawberry and Almond Cheesecake

SERVES 8

PREPARATION TIME 30 MINUTES

COOKING TIME 3 HOURS

CHILLING TIME 2 HOURS

INGREDIENTS

200 g / 7 oz / ¾ cup sweet oat biscuits,
  crushed

50 g / 1 ¾ oz / ¼ cup butter, melted

600 g / 1 lb 5 oz / 2 ¾ cups cream cheese

150 ml / 5 fl. oz / ⅔ cup soured cream

3 large eggs, plus 1 egg yolk

½ tsp almond essence

2 tbsp plain (all purpose) flour

150 g / 5 ½ oz / ⅔ cup caster (superfine) sugar

75 g / 2 ½ oz / 1 cup flaked (slivered) almonds

200 g / 7 oz / 1 ⅓ cups strawberries, quartered

METHOD

- Mix the biscuit crumbs with the butter and press into an even layer in the bottom of a spring-form cake tin that will fit inside your slow cooker.

- Whisk together the cream cheese, soured cream, eggs, egg yolk, almond essence, flour, sugar and flaked almonds until smoothly combined.

- Put a rack into the bottom of your slow cooker and add 2.5 cm (1 in) of boiling water, then position the cake tin on top. Cover the top of the slow cooker with 3 layers of kitchen paper before putting on the lid. The paper will collect the condensed steam and stop it from dripping onto the cheesecake.

- Cook on high for 2 hours, then turn off the slow cooker and leave to cook in the residual heat without lifting the lid for 1 hour.

- Take the cheesecake out of the slow cooker and leave to cool to room temperature before chilling for at least 2 hours. Pile the strawberries on top before serving.

TOP TIP

Try using stoned poached cherries in place of the strawberries.

Lavender and Honey Rice Pudding

SERVES 4

PREPARATION TIME 5 MINUTES

COOKING TIME 3 HOURS

INGREDIENTS

50 g / 1 ¾ oz / ¼ cup butter, plus extra for
  greasing
1.2 litres / 2 pints / 4 ½ cups whole milk
3 sprigs of lavender, stems removed
110 g / 4 oz / ½ cup short-grain rice
75 g / 2 ½ oz / ¼ cup runny honey, plus extra
  to serve

METHOD

- Butter the inside of a slow cooker.
  Stir all of the ingredients together,
  then tip the mixture into the
  slow cooker.

- Cook on high for 3 hours, stirring
  once every hour.

- Spoon into warm bowls and serve
  with extra honey for drizzling over.

TOP TIP
Try adding the finely
grated zest of an orange
for added zing.

Lemon Soufflés

SERVES 4
PREPARATION TIME 20 MINUTES
COOKING TIME 1 HOUR

INGREDIENTS

1 tbsp butter
3 tbsp caster (superfine) sugar
2 large egg whites
1 tbsp cornflour (cornstarch)
100 g / 3 ½ oz / ½ cup lemon curd

METHOD

- Put a rack inside a slow cooker and add 2.5 cm (1 in) of boiling water, then set it to high.

- Butter 4 mini pudding basins and use 1 tbsp of the sugar to coat the insides.

- Whisk the egg whites with an electric whisk until stiff, then whisk in the rest of the sugar. Stir the cornflour into the lemon curd, then fold in the egg whites.

- Spoon the mixture into the prepared pudding basins, then transfer them to the slow cooker. Lay 3 layers of kitchen paper over the top of the slow cooker before putting on the lid to absorb the condensed steam.

- Cook for 1 hour or until the soufflés are only just set in the centres. Serve immediately.

TOP TIP
Top with a scoop of vanilla ice cream and a drizzle of lemon curd before serving.

Slow-cooked knickerbocker glory

SERVES 6

PREPARATION TIME 10 MINUTES

COOKING TIME 1 HOUR 30 MINUTES

INGREDIENTS

1 pineapple, peeled and cut into chunks

300 g / 10 ½ oz / 1 ⅔ cups black
    cherries, stoned

3 pears, peeled, cored and cut into chunks

100 g / 3 ½ oz / ½ cup caster (superfine) sugar

100 ml / 3 ½ fl. oz / ½ cup rosé wine

6 scoops vanilla ice cream

50 g / 1 ¾ oz / ½ cup pistachio nuts, chopped

METHOD

- Mix the fruit with the sugar and wine
  in a slow cooker. Cover and cook on
  medium for 1 hour 30 minutes then
  leave to cool completely.

- Spoon the fruit and cooking liquor
  into 6 tall sundae glasses and top with
  the ice cream and pistachio nuts.

TOP TIP
Try serving with different
ice creams for
a change.

Carrot Cake

SERVES 10

PREPARATION TIME 25 MINUTES

COOKING TIME 3 HOURS

INGREDIENTS

175 g / 6 oz / 1 cup soft light brown sugar

2 large eggs

150 ml / 5 fl. oz / ⅔ cup sunflower oil

175 g / 6 oz / 1 ¼ cups plain (all purpose)
    flour

3 tsp baking powder

2 tsp ground cinnamon

1 orange, zest finely grated

200 g / 7 oz / 1 ⅔ cups carrots, washed and
    coarsely grated

100 g / 3 ½ oz / ¾ cup walnuts, chopped

FOR THE ICING

110 g / 4 oz / ½ cup cream cheese

55 g / 2 oz / ¼ cup butter, softened

110 g / 4 oz / 1 cup icing (confectioners')
    sugar

1 tsp vanilla extract

2 tbsp walnuts, finely chopped

METHOD

- Put a rack in the bottom of a slow cooker and add 2.5 cm (1 in) of boiling water. Grease and line a cake tin that will fit inside your slow cooker.

- Whisk the sugar, eggs and oil together for 3 minutes until thick. Fold in the flour, baking powder and cinnamon, followed by the orange zest, carrots and walnuts.

- Scrape the mixture into the tin and lower it into the slow cooker. Cook on high for 3 hours or until a skewer inserted in the centre comes out clean. Transfer the cake to a wire rack and leave to cool completely.

- To make the icing, beat the cream cheese and butter together with a wooden spoon until light and fluffy then beat in the icing sugar a quarter at a time. Add the vanilla extract then use a whisk to whip the mixture for 2 minutes or until smooth and light.

- Spread the icing over the cake and sprinkle with walnuts.

TOP TIP
Try using beetroot in place of the carrot.

Poached Pears and Cherries with Herbs

SERVES 6

PREPARATION TIME 5 MINUTES

COOKING TIME 2 HOURS

INGREDIENTS

4 pears, quartered

200 g / 7 oz / 1 ⅓ cups cherries, stoned and halved

2 tbsp caster (superfine) sugar

1 lemon, juiced

2 sprigs rosemary

2 sprigs thyme

METHOD

- Put everything in a slow cooker, then cover and cook on medium for 2 hours.

- Serve warm or chilled.

TOP TIP

Use the fruit as a base for a crumble or pie.

INDEX